A History of
FIGHTING SHIPS

A History of
FIGHTING SHIPS

Richard Hough

OCTOPUS

The text and illustrations in this book have been abridged from *Fighting Ships* by Richard Hough, which was originally published in Great Britain by Michael Joseph Ltd; in the United States of America, *Fighting Ships* was originally published by G.P. Putnam's Sons. *Fighting Ships* was designed and produced by George Rainbird Ltd, 44 Edgware Road, London W2.

ENDPAPERS: *Group of vessels by Van de Velde*
PAGE ONE: *Sails and driver of a 20-gun ship, by Steel*
PREVIOUS PAGES: *Dutch men of war and yacht, by Van de Velde II*
OPPOSITE: *The super-dreadnought, USS* Oklahoma, *1917*
OVERLEAF: *The Embarkation of Henry VIII at Dover*
PAGE 8: *The forward guns and bridge of the French cruiser,* Georges Leygues, *1937*

This edition first published 1975 by
Octopus Books Limited
59 Grosvenor Street, London W1

© Richard Hough 1969, 1975

ISBN 0 7064 0303 7

Distributed in Australia by
Rigby Limited
30 North Terrace, Kent Town,
Adelaide, South Australia 5067

Produced by Mandarin Publishers Limited
Westlands Road, Quarry Bay, Hong Kong

Printed in Hong Kong

+ + + + + + + + + + + +

Acknowledgments

The publishers would like to thank the owners, authorities and trustees of the following collections and museums for their kind permission to reproduce the illustrations in this book

Reproduced by Gracious Permission of Her Majesty the Queen: 6–7 (Hampton Court Palace, Photo: Cooper), 60
Alexandra Lawrence: 18 above, 57 below
Antikvarisk-topografiska Arkivet, Sweden: 22
Ashmolean Museum, Oxford: 30 above
Basil Taylor Esq: 67 below
Bettman Archive Inc., New York: 105 left
Bodleian Library, Oxford: 33 top and bottom left
British Museum: 29 below
George Bromley, M.S., F.R.C.S.: 92–93
Bundesarchiv, Germany: 126
Camera Press: jacket, 122 above
A W Carr: 24 below
'The Connoisseur': 44–45, 48 above
President and Fellows of Corpus Christi College, Oxford: 33 bottom right
Crown Copyright: 34 below, 113 above, 116–117, 124 below, 125 below
Derrick Witty: 41, 65, 72–73
Edward Leigh: 36, 40 above and below, 43 right, 46, 47, 54–55 above, 58 above
Galleria Doria, Rome: 37 above and below
'Illustrated Penny Almanack' for 1879: 110 centre
Imperial War Museum: 106–107, 110–111 above centre, below and above right, 118, 119, 120–121 below, 133, 134–135 above, 139
Jacqueline Hyde: 52, 56, 58 below, 63, 76 above and below
John Freeman: 25 below, 29 above, 49, 101
Laurence Dunn: 8
Master and Fellows of Magdalene College, Cambridge: 36, 40 above and below, 43 right, 46, 47, 54–55 above, 58 above
Mansell Collection: 11, 12, 13, 21 centre, 24–25 above, 42 left, 105 right

Mariners Museum, Newport News, Virginia: 67 above right
Maritiem Museum Prins Hendrik, Rotterdam: 28
Mr and Mrs Paul Mellon: 64, 70 above
Musée de la Marine, Paris: 19 above, 52, 56, 58 below, 63, 76 above and below
National Maritime Museum, Greenwich: 2–3, 10, 23, 26 below, 27 above and below, 39 above, 41, 42–43, 51, 62, 65, 68, 69 below, 72–73, 77 (Greenwich Hospital Collection), 78, 79, 83, 84 above, 86 above, 86–87 below, 87 above, 89, 91, 95, 96, 97 above and below, 106 left, 110 above, 128
Oscar and Peter Johnson Limited, Lowndes Lodge Gallery: 69 above
Palazzo Ducale, Venice: 14–15 below
Radio Times Hulton Picture Library: 5, 17, 94, 138
Rijksmuseum, Holland: 35, 50, 61
Rupert Preston Gallery: 90
Rutland Gallery: 124–125 above
San Martino, Naples: 14–15 above
Scala: endpapers, 10, 14–15 above and below, 37 above and below
Schleswig-Holsteinisches Landesmuseum, Germany: 21 above
Science Museum: 1, 9, 16, 26 above, 30 below, 32 above and below, 54 below, 55 below, 57 above, 59, 67 above left and centre, 70 below, 71 above, 74, 75, 98–99, 100, 103 above and below, 104, 107 right, 109, 112 left and below right, 115 (lent by C Cochrane & Co., Birkenhead), 120 above, 121 above, 123, 132, 134–135 below, 136
Sjöhistoriska Museum Wasavarvet, Sweden: 53 above and below
Society of Antiquaries: 38–39
Universitet i Bergen Historisk Museum, Norway: 21 below
official US Navy photo: 80–81, 82, 84 below, 85 above and below, 88, 113 below, 122 below, 127, 129, 131, 137, 140, 141
Victoria and Albert Museum: 18 above, 18–19 below (Ham House), 31, 34 above, 57 below
Woburn Abbey Collection (with kind permission of His Grace the Duke of Bedford): 48 below

CONTENTS

PREFACE

*Ever since the days of Phoenician sea Power, the fighting
ship has been the noblest and most splendid of all the weapons of
war, inspiring reassurance and courage in those who sailed
in it. Unlike the tank and military aircraft, the fighting ship has
always possessed in its design a measure of both the
functional and the decorative. The loving skill of the artist, matched
by the practical wisdom of the shipwright, can result in
an object of peerless beauty. When a Humphreys-designed frigate
sails in all its elegance from the mouth of the Delaware,
when a great Dreadnought of this century fires a full broadside at
30 knots, the proof is complete that the fighting ship is one
of history's most beautiful and fearful creations.*

*The visual quality of men-of-war, then, is something to be
cherished, and a fully illustrated history of the fighting ship through
the ages a worthwhile object. The number and range of
illustrations has demanded an economy of text which
has represented something of a challenge. The subject of naval
architecture and development is so vast that this book
cannot attempt to be much more than a summary of the most
important trends and developments.*

Richard Hough

Chapter One

THE OAR-DRIVEN FIGHTING SHIP

The fighting ship propelled mainly by man's muscles had a life span of some 4,500 years, longer by far than that of the sailing fighting ship. It also developed through more forms than the sailing warship, or than the steam-powered warship, which has lasted for little more than a century.

Egyptian Origins

The Mediterranean, 'the cradle of oversea traffic and of the art of naval combats', as Conrad has described it, has seen more sea fighting than any other ocean in the world. There is evidence of a great sea battle between the Egyptians and the 'peoples of the north' around the time of the Trojan wars. In the Mediterranean Antony deserted his fleet at Actium, Nelson lost an eye and gained one of his greatest victories, and torpedo-bombers of the British navy signalled the end of the heavy gunned fighting ship 140 years later at Taranto. The cradle of the fighting ship was almost certainly the estuary of the Nile; and sea warfare began when bold armed mariners in strengthened river craft ventured forth into open waters for the first time – to explore, to pillage, perhaps to trade, and certainly to confront new enemies.

The nature of the earliest sea fighting, and the form and characteristics of the vessels, are likely to remain obscure for ever. One of the few valuable

ABOVE: *Bas relief of an Egyptian rowing boat from the tomb of Ti near Saqqara* c. *2650 BC*

OPPOSITE: *Detail of 'Portuguese carracks off a rocky coast', 1521, by Anthoniszoon, showing oars grouped in threes*

sources of knowledge of the early Egyptian fighting ship is the relief carvings on one of the Abu Sir pyramids, which have been dated at about 2600 BC, and fragments of detailed reliefs dating from Pharaoh Sahure (2700 BC). These show a Nile river type of vessel with bipod mast, upright stem and stern posts. The fourteen oarsmen are shown standing for greater purchase, and the mast is lowered onto a crutch as evidence that the wind is unfavourable for sailing.

There is little evidence of any radical improvement or elaboration on this primitive strengthened river vessel for the next 1000 years or so. By 1500 BC the oar remained the principal means of power.

Some 300 years later, as tribes from the south coasts of Asia Minor and the southern Aegean islands engaged in sporadic but well organized raids against the Phoenician and Egyptian coasts, there took place the first naval battle of which there is pictorial evidence. This great unidentified sea battle, between the Egyptians and the marauding 'Northmen of the Mediterranean', was fought fiercely at close range mainly with bows-and-arrows, slings and spears. It marks the decline of the Egyptian warship.

The Galley

From 1100 to 800 BC, the chief initiative and enterprise in maritime power passed to the Phoenicians. They were responsible for the warship as a distinct species, rather than as a trading vessel modified and equipped to carry troops.

Up to about 700 BC the oar-driven Mediterranean fighting ship was powered by a single bank of oars on each beam, each oar operated by a single oarsman, standing or sitting. The first evidence of the galley with oars in two banks and at two levels – the *bireme* – has been found on Assyrian reliefs evidently depicting Phoenician fighting ships of around 700 BC. The fighting men occupy a 'storming bridge', a narrow deck like a gallery, extending the full length of the vessel above the inboard oarsmen. A wicked-looking ram, projecting some eight to twelve feet forward from the bows like the horn of a charging rhinoceros, is the vessel's main 'armament', the real killing weapon which may, at some seven knots, slice clean through an enemy ship. A single square sail is still only an auxiliary means of propulsion.

The most famous vessel of ancient times is the Greek *trireme*, which dominated the Battle of Salamis in 480 BC. The arrangement of oars and oarsmen has for long been the subject of controversy among naval historians. There was probably no standard seating and rowing arrangement; this – like the formation of the hull design, the construction of the prow and many other features – varied widely over the years and at any given time. History is never a very tidy business, and there is no more reason for an Athenian trireme fighting off the Arginusae islands in 406 BC to be identical to one of Ptolemy's a hundred years later than that identical features should mark, say, the design of French and American frigates in AD 1812. It is very likely, too, that even the commonly accepted number of 170 oarsmen – thirty-one each side on the upper bank and twenty-seven a side on each of the two lower banks – was not rigidly adhered to in the Greek trireme.

Naval fighting in the Mediterranean in the 400 years before the birth of Christ was mainly conducted by Carthaginians and Greeks, Phoenicians, Macedonians and Romans, who all brought sea fighting to a higher degree of refinement than was to be seen again until many centuries later. The vessels that fought – whether biremes, triremes or perhaps quin-

queremes – might be between 60 and 120 feet long with a beam of 10 to 20 feet. The ram, whether of hard, sheathed wood made to detach under violent impact, or integral with the galley's hull, remained the primary weapon of destruction, although the Romans tended to despise tactical finesse and relied more on their larger complement of soldiers and the bludgeoning weight of the boarding party.

Fire was another effective killer at a range, but this was a clumsy weapon which endangered the user almost as seriously as his enemy. The sailors of Rhodes in the third century BC made effective use of containers of fire projecting from the bows on long poles like the spar torpedoes used by the Americans in the Civil War. When conditions were favourable, blazing rafts were sometimes floated towards a trapped enemy. The most effective recorded instance of the use of fire as a weapon is at Actium, in the last frightful stages of the holocaust, when Agrippa had already torn apart by ram the remnants of Antony's fleet.

'The assailants coming from many sides,' records Dio Cassius, 'shot blazing missiles and with engines threw pots of flaming charcoal and pitch. The defendants tried to ward off these fiery projectiles and

when one lodged it was quenched with drinking water. When that was gone, they dipped up sea water, but as their buckets were small and few and half-filled they were not always successful. They smothered the fires with their mantles and even with corpses. They hacked off burning parts of the ships and tried to grapple hostile ships to escape into them. Many were burned alive or jumped overboard or killed each other to avoid the flames.'

Fire, the ultimate terror at sea, was decisive at Actium and it was an important weapon of Howard at Calais 1,600 years later during the Armada engagement. But it remained a hit-or-miss business in ancient times, used only occasionally, until the Byzantine Romans perfected 'Greek fire' – a form of liquid bitumen which at short range was blown by giant bellows through copper tubes and was only further activated by water.

The Venetians

The Galie Subtile.

Tunnage._____ 200.
Menn { Marrynars. 242 } 250.
{ Gonnars _____ 8 }

It says much for the early Mediterranean naval architects that their form of oar-driven fighting ship remained basically unchanged for another fifteen or more centuries after the birth of Christ. The power and speed varied with the size of the vessel and the number and disposition of the oarsmen, the introduction of the lateen sail made possible the more frequent use of the capricious Mediterranean winds, the cannon was introduced and influenced the design and destructive potential. But in overall concept there was little to choose between a dromon of the first century and a galley of the 1700s, in spite of all the ingenuity of the Venetian builders.

Venice was the most maritime-conscious nation in the Mediterranean for more than five hundred years, and for most of this period the Venetians led the way in the small variations in design of the fighting galley. Biremes following the basic pattern of the Roman galleys centuries earlier remained the most common vessel until the latter part of the fourteenth century.

Then, with the growing need for more powerful and more numerous guns, the Mediterranean galley began again to increase in size and complexity, just as the iron-clad and steel-clad battleships of the nineteenth and twentieth centuries became more elaborate and formidable with the increasing range and destructive power of contemporary artillery. And as the need for greater speed to meet the tactical demands of battle and the greater displacement of the hull caused the horsepower of the twentieth-century battleship to rise from 12,000 to 220,000, so more oarsmen had to be accommodated. The displacement was about 170 tons and the overall length had increased to 165 feet from the tip of the prow to the extremity of the raised and carved poop, and the beam at the waterline was 18 feet. Within these dimensions there was housed a total complement of 225 men, the oarsmen working on askew benches in groups of three, each with a single oar weighing about 125 pounds. It is no wonder that the stroke was a slow one, no more than 26 a minute at racing speeds, which with a following wind, under the most

OPPOSITE: *The galie subtile from the Anthony Anthony Roll, 1546, manned by 242 'Marrynars' and 8 'Gonnars', and of some 200 tons displacement*

BELOW: *An early seventeenth-century galley, which later developed into the reale, by Furttenbach. There are 27 oars a side, each pulled by five oarsmen*

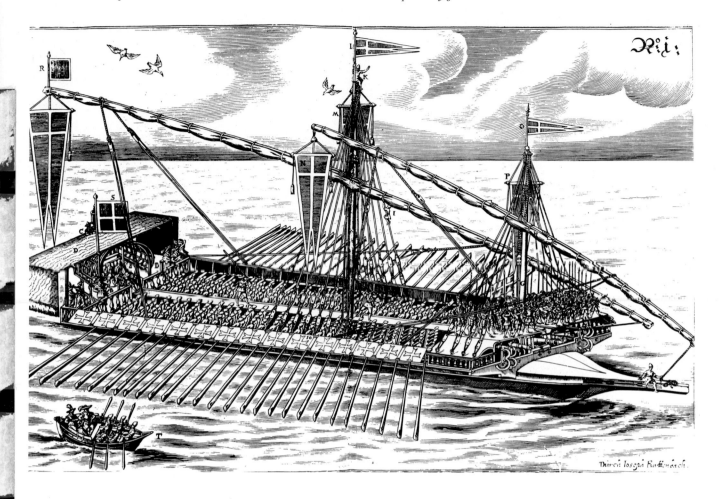

favourable conditions and for a brief spurt only, might rise to 12 knots. All the oarsmen rose together from their seats, placing a foot on the bench ahead to gain leverage and inserting their blades as far forward as possible. Then they would all laboriously draw on the oar, falling back slowly into their seats as they did so. A gong, or perhaps a primitive band, would provide encouragement and the beat. Most Mediterranean states used captured Turkish slaves, and these were chained to their benches. The Venetians retained the old practice of using freemen, who were provided with arms, so that fewer permanent soldiers had to be carried. Whether Turkish, Genoese, Spanish or Venetian, the fighting galley was an evil-smelling vessel and conditions on board were fearful.

Besides the five forward-mounted guns, these highly-developed mid-sixteenth-century galleys carried perhaps half a dozen light 3-pounder guns on pivot mounts on each side, and the slow revolution gunpowder was bringing about in the whole nature of

the fighting ship was further evidenced in the provision of arquebuses and muskets in place of bows and arrows for close-range action.

The Galleass

Before wind-power took over from the oar-driven vessel – with all its wretched human misery – there was a period of unsatisfactory compromise comparable with the era of mixed sail and steam motive power in the second half of the nineteenth century. Out of the need of the fighting seamen for more guns and bigger guns, and the need to flee or pursue or manoeuvre in battle, there grew the hybrid *galleass*. The galleass was a greatly enlarged galley, carrying a very large number of guns and with its oar-power augmented normally by three lateen-rigged masts. It was the capital ship of its day. It grew out of the heavy merchantmen, the *galia grosa*, which plied its trade in the Mediterranean from the 1400s, protected against marauders by a small number of light guns.

17

ABOVE: *'The Venetian galeass', by Gueroult. Its origins were again Mediterranean, a sea where the disparity between the development of the gun and the means to bring it to bear on the enemy was most marked because of the uncertainty of wind as motive power*

RIGHT: *The Battle of Lepanto, 1571, by an anonymous sixteenth-century Venetian painter. Some 230 galleys, galleasses and other vessels of the combined fleets of Spain, Malta, Venice and the Vatican fought an even larger concourse of Turkish vessels, from dawn until just before midnight on 7 October*

OPPOSITE *(above)*: *A model of the reale* Dauphine *from the end of the seventeenth century with twenty-six pairs of thwarts and five men to each oar. The most sumptuous reales were decorated with carving by Pierre Pugin; their most famous action was Matapan in 1717*

For its conversion to a fighting rôle the artillery of this merchantman was augmented with a heavy battery consisting perhaps of six 36-pounders firing forward and three 24-pounders to fire on the broadside.

The broadside armament carried on each side would also normally be increased. These converted galleasses, with their additional weight of guns and fighting men, were even slower than they had been as merchantmen.

The last great battle in which galleys or galleasses took part was off Cape Matapan in 1717, and only a handful were built in later years. The summit of their achievements occurred nearly a century and a half earlier. At Lepanto, fought off the coast of Greece in 1571, some 230 galleys, galleasses and other vessels of the combined fleets of Spain, Malta, Venice and the Vatican fought an even larger concourse of Turkish vessels, from dawn until just before midnight on 7 October. Maritime power at sea, in the finest hours of the oar-driven fighting ship, was fully to justify itself in the cause of Christianity, for a Turkish victory must have changed the course of history throughout Europe. The six Venetian galleasses played an important rôle, their firepower proving decisive.

The Vikings

While the genesis of the Mediterranean galley lay in the primitive papyrus rafts of the Nile and the Tigris, the ancestors of the Viking longship were crudely hollowed-out tree trunks used on the lakes, rivers and fjords of Scandinavia. Papyrus rafts of a design believed to be identical to those of the prehistoric age are built today on the Nile and other African rivers, and dugouts were still being hewn in the more remote regions of Finland in this century. The climate of the north may have its drawbacks, but at least for the purpose of tracing the development of boat design it is not necessary to rely on fragments of carvings and the coloured accounts of contemporary poets. The preservative qualities of the mud and clay of marshlands, river estuaries and poorly-drained fields have yielded up numerous examples of northern boat design, from the most simple hollowed-out tree trunk to near-complete Viking fighting ships, which had sometimes been ceremonially buried and then discovered centuries later in excellent condition by delighted archaeologists.

Until recent times, the characteristics of the fighting ship have been closely related to its local climate and geographical environment. The Viking long-ship, lean, robust, with fine seagoing and sailing qualities, was the ideal man-of-war for the northern warrior travelling on his long-distance raids in the storm-racked waters of the North Sea and Atlantic. The Viking's fighting ship never matched the fighting qualities of the contemporary Roman galley, but the fierce weather of the north with its long swells would soon have smashed the frail Mediterranean trireme; and no southern vessel could equal the sailing qualities of its northern counterpart. In the north, the wind was the prime motive power, and centuries before the coming of the Viking longship, the northern sailor had mastered the art of close-hauling and sailing into the wind.

Viking restlessness, the subsequent raiding and then massive colonization which spread throughout most of northern Europe, had its origins in the discovery in Scandinavia of great supplies of readily available iron ore. With the tools wrought from this new mineral, agriculture flourished and the population increased rapidly – so rapidly that efforts to feed the hungry began to fail. Fishing was one answer to the problem, and this led to the application of greater skills to the art of ship design. The need for new lands to colonize became critical, and by AD 700 the practice of raiding across the North Sea and beyond was firmly established. At first the vessels were fighting

ABOVE: *The Nydam ship, fourth century, is thought to have had stones for ballast and a bottom board rather than a keel. Tacitus described this type of ship: 'Clinker-built, oak, riveted, V-shaped'*

RIGHT: *The figurehead of a Viking ship. It is interesting to compare this with the carved Norman prows*

OPPOSITE: *The Gökstad ship, tenth century, had sixteen oars a side. She is built up from a heavy external keel to a high stem and stern post, to which the ribbing is secured by planking adjacent to the keel. The other seven lower planks are lashed through lugs to the ribs, while the upper ones are nailed direct by iron spikes. All the strakes overlap (clinker-built) and are clench-nailed and caulked with tarred ropes. Two feet above the top of the keel and secured to the ribs on either side are the beams, which support the decking. Some 18 inches below the gunwhale are the 16 oar-ports, each sealed with a cap*

BELOW: *A thirteenth-century wood carving of a fleet of Viking-type ships in battle order*

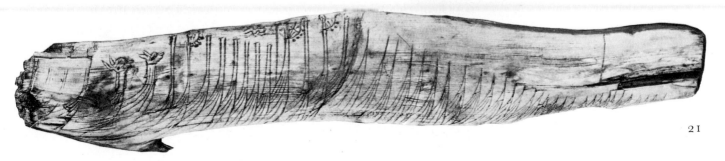

21

ships, and battle was the chief occupation of those who sailed in them. From these were developed the fierce and beautiful longships which sailed on those remarkable voyages of discovery to Iceland and Greenland and to the Continent of America. Only in the later Viking period were ships built primarily for transporting colonists with their families and tools. These vessels, the *knorrs*, were constructed with a wider beam and flatter bottom, and relied even more than the longships on the wind for propulsion.

It is the famous Gökstad ship on which we mainly rely for exact details of the construction of the Viking longship in its ultimate form, although it is known that vessels designed for extended seagoing trips were considerably larger. The almost completely preserved Gökstad ship of AD 900 was found in a 15-foot-high burial mound of blue clay on a farm near Sande Fjord in Norway in 1880, and today can be seen, fully restored, in Oslo. Constructed entirely of oak, and skilfully fashioned by the new iron tools, it probably weighed 20 tons when fully laden for sea. The vessel would have been built on land and launched on rollers into shallow water. The Gökstad ship was a

modest-sized fighting ship for its time. As proof of her seagoing qualities, a replica of the ship was built in 1893 and sailed across the Atlantic for the World's Fair at Chicago and the four hundredth anniversary of the 'discovery' of America. She made the passage without mishap, proving herself capable of a speed of 11 knots under sail.

Sea fighting among the Norsemen was a fierce and brutish business, with little skill or subtlety. As in the early days of Roman power, it was nothing more than land combat transferred to the precarious uncertainty of narrow vessels of war, and conducted wherever possible in sheltered waters. It was fought with swords and spears and fearful great axes. As in the Mediterranean, an action was opened at a distance with volleys of stones and arrows – the Viking was a specially fine bowman. But the elaborate tactical evolution on which the Mediterranean sailor prided himself, and the ram which governed these manoeuvrings, were unknown in the north. The longships were sometimes lashed together for mutual protection, from that point in any combat the situation became nothing more than a furious mêlée.

OPPOSITE: *The Battle of The Saints, 1782, was Rodney's great victory over the French. The sailing warship nears the limit of its development at this time*

BELOW: *The Gotland pictorial stones of the seventh and eighth centuries*

Chapter Two

THE SAILING FIGHTING SHIP

Prelude to the Three-master

Until recently, the oceans of the world have been thought hostile and mysterious, and at best the relationship between man and the sea has been an uneasy one, in which anxiety and superstition have thrived. It is no wonder that the development of the fighting ship from its earliest days has been retarded by caution and traditionalism. The sailor has always hated change of any kind; and the taming of the wind to the needs of the long-distance mariner was therefore a long and arduous process. But at length the means by which a ship could be sailed efficiently close to and into the wind was discovered, and accepted by the sailor. Thus the inception of the three-master was brought about. It was a slow business, and it was not achieved until Western man had emerged from the Dark Ages, and had begun to enjoy the security at home which, paradoxically, has always sent him off in fighting ships to conquer and then to colonize. The three-masted ship opened up the world and brought about the great age of discovery and exploration. It also revolutionized the fighting ship and sea warfare. Until the fighting sailor, with the three-master, was able to sail in all weathers and to all places, and the gunsmith had mastered his craft, sea fighting remained essentially a matter of hand-to-hand combat carried out in quiet waters close to

shore. Among the weapons used, only the ram brought about any degree of tactical elaboration, for the purpose of missiles, arrows and spears, and even molten lead and liquid fire, was to strike fear and injury among the foe before sword, muscle, and courage brought about a decision. In sea fighting the quality of the man always counted above the quality of the *matériel*, but never more so than during the two thousand years that separated the period of Phoenician maritime power from the Battle of Sluys in 1340.

By the standards of later progress, little happened to the fighting ship between the arrival of the Duke of Normandy in Pevensey Bay for the conquest of England in 1066 and the departure of Christopher Columbus from Palos for America in 1492. But the fact that Columbus could even contemplate such a long and hazardous journey – and without oars – is evidence that the ship had become an ocean-going means of transport. For fighting, the ship had also acquired cannon. By the late 1400s, then, a new age of battle at sea had opened. Suddenly, the fighting ship could sail for thousands of miles, hover off an enemy coast, blockade, strike at targets ashore, manoeuvre freely and engage an enemy in the open sea. The fighting ship had grown up, and was not to change fundamentally for another 400 years.

William of Normandy may or may not have had oars in his ships. But he *sailed* to conquer England. The single-masted warship continued to dominate northern waters for many years after the invasion, and the heavy oars carried aboard were resorted to only in a rare calm. Evidence of the shape and form of ships of the 1100s and 1200s is derived almost entirely from the contemporary seals of the northern ports. The artists had a hard time portraying a long ship on a small, round piece of metal; and, while it is certain that seagoing vessels were constructed more stubbily as the sail took over from the oar, they still owed much to the Viking longship, and the seals show a deceptively foreshortened hull.

The traditional configuration of the three-master, with high castle fore and aft, originated in the eastern Mediterranean, and came north with the return from the Crusades, and from engagements with Saracen men-of-war, of sailors who found themselves at a crippling disadvantage in their Viking type single-masters. From these Saracen ships stemmed the vessels of Columbus and Vasco da Gama, Magellan and Drake.

The Fighting Ship as a Gun-platform

From around 1400, widening curiosity about the world – and the subsequent conflicts of interest – brought about notable advances in the science of navigation and exploration, and of combat at sea, as well as in the ships themselves. As the ship grew to meet the mariners' needs, a true comprehension of the means to propel it more safely and efficiently on any desired course spread among all the European ship designers. This was the century not only of the three-master, but also of the compass and the gun. America was rediscovered, the world was circumnavigated, and the shape of the ship was changed for ever. The fighting ship began to take on an exclusive warlike rôle and characteristics of its own. No longer could those bent on war rely entirely on recalling the vessels from peaceful trade and fit them out with soldiers and a handful of primitive missile-

RIGHT: *The English fleet from the Bayeux tapestry*

OPPOSITE: *The French fleet from the Bayeux tapestry*

The Bayeux tapestry provides strong evidence that the graceful, single-masted, clinker-built, Gökstad-style vessel, with its sharp sheer forward and aft leading up to a high stem and stern-post, spread to all northern regions washed by the Atlantic, the North Sea and the Baltic.
In King Harold's ship, and others, the lady embroiderers have included the oar-ports – sixteen a side as in the Gökstad ship. William the Conqueror's ship in which he landed in England in 1066 is under its single sail, and the oar-ports are not shown. It has a brightly painted and decorated sail, a carved figurehead at the prow and a cross at the masthead which indicates the Pope's approval of the invasion

BELOW: *The Belgian font of Winchester Cathedral showing a ship with a mid-twelfth-century rudder*

24

throwers. Henceforward, naval power was to be wielded more and more by standing fleets of fighting ships.

Pictorial evidence of the advent of the three-master in the north has been discovered in a manuscript dated around 1450, and a three-masted ship is clearly depicted on a seal struck for Louis XI in 1466. There can be no doubt that by the second half of the century all large sea-going vessels constructed in northern Europe, in Spain, Portugal, and the Mediterranean, carried three masts. With its fundamental advantages now recognized everywhere in Europe, development went ahead apace, and before the end of the century numerous refinements had been introduced. The most important was the spritsail. The bowsprit had not been used as a spar since the days of the Roman artemon. Now that – at last – the benefits to be derived from a sail far forward were again becoming appreciated, the next step was simple. The spritsail was rigged *under* the bowsprit, where it proved its worth as a headsail more effectively than the earlier foresail. What was more, the foremast could now be used to carry a driving sail – at first a small one be-

cause of the mast's inadequate support in its forward position, but soon to grow larger as its mast was stepped farther aft. By 1498 Vasco da Gama was actually able to hoist a small fore-topsail.

The gunsmith, too, had been busy throughout the century. The influence of his works was to be profound and long-lasting. Until the 1300s, the means of destroying the enemy in sea warfare were limited: at a distance, to various forms of missile and – much more rarely – to fire; at close quarters to the common hand-weapons of the time. Only the ancient ram and, again very rarely, fire had served as ship destroyers. All this was to be changed by the discovery of a diabolical compound of charcoal, saltpetre and sulphur, and the means of harnessing its ignition through the medium of a cylinder. It was not a neat, quick revolution; like all great developments in the fighting ship up to the 1900s, the refinement and acceptance of the gun, even from a sort of cast bowl to a cylinder, took a long time. From what we know about the operation and effect of the earliest guns, the fighting sailor's preference for the bow or sling, *trébuchet* or ballista can be understood. The gun was a clumsy, heavy, inefficient, highly dangerous weapon, and it says much for the courage of the mariner of the 1300s and 1400s that he allowed it on board his ship at all.

It is not possible to date for sure within ten or twenty years when the first gun was taken on board. There is some evidence that the French, Genoese and English used them to add to the holocaust at Sluys. It is possible that the Venetians and Genoese – the most farsighted seamen – used them before the 1340s; certainly they fought each other with them in the 1370s. There is documentary evidence, in the Public Record Office, that English ships carried a modest armament of guns in 1411. But long before that, in 1345, King Henry IV's ship *Christopher* sported '*iii cannons de ferr ove v. chambres, un handgone, un petit barrell de gonpouder, le quart plein*', and the Keeper of the

25

King's Wardrobe was honoured – surely to his surprise and alarm – with the task of looking after ships' guns and keeping them supplied with powder and shot.

These early ship guns, employed in combat by all the European maritime nations by the middle 1400s, were only man-destroyers. They were small, light, few in number, and probably regarded as rather novel and dashing, if only because it called for exceptional courage to fire the charge. No doubt, however, they provided the moral reinforcement in the man behind the breech and the fear in the man facing the muzzle that the naval gun has instilled right down to the 16- and 18-inch weapons of the 1940s. These early ship-borne cannon, unlike the cast pieces used in land warfare in the 1300s, were built up from a number of forged iron strips welded together longitudinally about a cylindrical tube and reinforced at first with a wood case or a wound rope, and later with shrunk-on iron hoops. A typical light *petarara* of the 1470s was some 3 feet long and weighed around 120 pounds. A trunnion secured to the barrel could be locked into a swivel post by fork extensions curving up each side of the breech, drilled to carry a horizontal securing pin, which provided the gunner with the means to adjust the elevation for range. The breech piece was hollowed out to slide over the rear end of the barrel and to receive the separate chamber which had been pre-loaded with powder and ball shot and was dropped in by a fixed handle. A wedge through the breech piece was driven home and forced the chamber up against the barrel. A light at the end of a long stick was then applied to the touch-hole, accompanied at first by prayers but soon by a show of self-confidence. The calibre of this light gun might be 2 or 3 inches, the weight of the ball little more than a pound, and the effective range no more than that of an arrow. It would make no effect on the structure of a ship, but fired into a crowd could kill one or more of the enemy and frighten the rest. With reserve chambers ready charged, the rate of fire was quite rapid, until the barrel became too hot.

As these light pieces of artillery increasingly proved their effectiveness during the late 1400s, the natural prejudice against them diminished and the fighting seamen demanded more. At first these were sited on each side of the two castles, the traditional station of the missile thrower, and also to fire down into the low waist of their own ship where boarders were likely to secure their first foothold – for, until the perfection of ship-destroying artillery, combat at sea remained essentially a man-to-man business with the capture of the enemy vessel the main target, and no ship could

ABOVE: *The seal of Hythe, Kent, showing a late twelfth- or early thirteenth-century ship. Seals of Continental ports, and of the Cinque ports – Hythe, Dover, Romney, Sandwich and Hastings – offer most of the evidence about early ship construction, although such evidence is often unreliable*

BELOW: *The seal of Sandwich showing a late thirteenth- or early fourteenth-century ship. This seal shows that Viking principles were still being followed – clinker construction, heavy sheer fore and aft, high stem and stern-posts, a single pole mast stepped amidships with a square sail*

ABOVE: *An impression of the seal of John, Duke of Bedford, warden of the Cinque ports of about 1426. This seal shows clearly the development of both the forecastles and aftercastles, which had become higher and stronger; the actual representation is a little crude*

BELOW: *The seal of Dover of 1305 shows that the typical English fighting ship has heavier and more elaborate castles, and there is a top-castle for the lookout to sight the enemy and the archers and slingers to use in battle. The steersman's oar is shown on the port side*

be taken as a prize until the castles had been stormed and the men overcome. Later, a few guns were disposed low down in the waist, and were protected by an additional heavy plank which became known as the gunwale; but the castles, with their commanding situation, made much the best sites. More and more of these light railing-pieces were added until they jammed both castles, which in turn had to be extended towards the centre of the ship. When even this proved inadequate accommodation, a second deck was added above the first, and filled with more guns, the spaces between the lower guns being planked in for protection of the gunners, thus forming the first gun embrasures. Then a third deck to each castle was added, and now it could truly be said that the gun – even the light man-destroying gun – had proved itself. By the end of the 1400s it must have shown itself to be a real killer and reasonably reliable. Although no ship had yet been sunk as a result of the introduction of gunpowder, in its design and shape the fighting ship was already bending to the needs of its own gunpower.

For the next four centuries the man-of-war, which until so recently had been just a troop transport, became more and more a floating gun platform. Speed, manoeuvrability and power to resist the elements had figured largely in the minds of naval architects since the Phoenicians. All these characteristics would continue to be important; but henceforward the fighting prowess of the warship would rest on the guns – their number, their reliability, their accuracy and rate of fire. The gun had won over all the missiles, and its fearful thunder would shape the form and character of the fighting ship until the new underwater weapons of modern times threatened its dominance.

Guns also brought new strains and stresses to the hull of the fighting ship, and new constructional problems for the shipwright. It was not possible to cut a series of holes in the side of a ship without weakening the structure, or to introduce several rows of guns each weighing a ton or more plus their ammunition without creating an adverse effect on the balance of the vessel. To meet the demands of these new weights and stresses, the northern shipbuilder was forced at last to conform with ancient Mediterranean practice and to resort to flush planking, or carvel construction, with each plank butting up against those above and below it. This was not only much stronger but made the cutting of the gunports a simpler operation for the carpenter. Clinker building of heavy ships, with the strakes overlapping, had all but ceased by 1525. With the introduction of more than a single line of

ABOVE: 'The Battle of Zonchio', 1499, an anonymous sixteenth-century Venetian school woodcut, which is probably the earliest extant print of a definite historical sea fight

OPPOSITE: The Catalan ship. A contemporary carving of a fifteenth-century caravel, made as a thank-offering by a sailor to

the Virgin. It shows the separated triangular poop and small raised stern deck, and is the type of ship used by Columbus

BELOW: A dramatic portrayal of a sea battle from an early fourteenth-century manuscript, showing clearly the functions of the forecastle and aftercastle as platforms for the fighting men

ABOVE: 'St Nicholas rebuking the tempest', by Bicci di Lorenzo, an early fifteenth-century Italian painter

LEFT: A Mediterranean carrack of the late fifteenth century, a vessel of both trade and war of which little is known for sure. In the early 1300s it was probably a dumpy round-ended merchantman with a single mast raked forward and carrying a single lateen sail. As the southern traders became more adventurous in their voyages, European influence was absorbed. The lateen sail was dropped in favour of the square sail although a small mizzen mast carrying a lateen sail was used, probably because the southern seamen found the square sail difficult to manage. As ships with two and even three masts had been used in the Mediterranean for many generations, this step would not be regarded with the wonder and caution of the northern sailor

OPPOSITE: A Portuguese ship painted on an early fifteenth-century Hispano-Moresque bowl, showing a third mast set well forward and carrying a single square sail acting as a head-sail and giving an entirely new sense of balance. This classic sail arrangement endured for centuries

gunports, it also became necessary to bring the upper line as close to the centre of the ship as possible in order to reduce the effect of excessive top weight. The shipwright accomplished this by curving in the side of the vessel at a distance above the waterline – a convex form as seen in the cross-section that came to be known as *the tumble-home* – so that the upper line of guns was set back from the lower line. The greatest beam of the ship was therefore just below the lower gun deck.

Of even greater importance, the heavy gun and its port signalled the end of the medieval round ship. While the merchantman continued to act the oc-

casional rôle of fighting ship between its customary peaceful duties of cargo-carrying, and while ships were boarded in battle rather than battered from a distance, it seemed sensible to construct them for maximum capacity. By the early 1500s, with the final disappearance of the merchantman's double function (though of course right up to the Napoleonic wars and even to the great wars of the 1900s merchantmen were pressed into combat service with the addition of a few guns) the dimensions of the fighting ship could be made solely to meet the needs of the battle.

At the beginning of the reign of Henry VIII the ratio of length to beam of his ships was about two to one; before his death it had increased to more than three to one. Both speed and handiness were thus gained by this reversion to hull proportions more closely comparable to those of the Viking longship and the Mediterranean galley. But the sterns of these new vessels bore no resemblance to those earlier fighting ships. They were cut off squarely by a wide athwartships transom, and the fighting power, especially in the event of a stern chase, was further increased by the addition of a stern armament of several heavy cannon.

It is one of the happy coincidences of history that the reign of Henry VIII spanned a dramatically important phase in the history of the fighting ship, for this English monarch was at once an enthusiastic navalist and an advocate of the heavy gun. Not for another 300 years was there to be a comparable period of advancement in the fighting ship and its gunpower, and his influence on this, by building up a navy of great power and by his enthusiastic interest in all maritime matters, was long-lasting. At the beginning of his reign there was constructed the appropriately named and famous *Henry Grace à Dieu*; before he died he had created the prototype of the ship-of-the-line which was to save England from Spanish rule and endure in developed form until the coming of iron and steam in the 1850s. The startling progress made in less than forty years is seen in the modifications to the first of these ships and the hull form, rig and armament of the second.

The Spanish, Portuguese and French especially were building very large carrack-like men-of-war early in the 1500s and one of the most formidable of these was the *Great Michael*, built in France for the King of Scotland.

ABOVE: *A model of a fifteenth-century Flemish carrack seen from above, showing the deck arrangement. The grappling hook, shields, and the spears in the mast-castles indicate that this carrack was used in time of war*

LEFT: *The seal of Southampton, clearly showing the three masts and bowsprit together with the rigging. The guns at the open gunport indicate that this was a fighting vessel*

OPPOSITE *(above)*: *'The Argonauts land at Colchis', from a fifteenth-century French manuscript*

OPPOSITE *(below left)*: *A sixteenth-century manuscript picture thought to show a contemporary English ship. Only two masts are in evidence and there is no sign of a bowsprit although bowsprits have been used as spars carrying a spritsail rigged below them as a headsail since the second half of the fifteenth century*

OPPOSITE *(below right)*: *'Henry I's nightmare', from a twelfth-century English manuscript*

Early Guns

Ship-destroying guns were slow to make their appearance on board because their weight and size and unpredictable performance made them a poor risk. The formidable recoil of a land gun that could destroy the wall of a castle might well, it was calculated, fatally injure the structure of a ship. Light man-destroyers came to be increasingly well-regarded but for some 150 years after their introduction had no fundamental influence on naval tactics. The development of heavy artillery, for use on land as well as at sea, depended on securing the breech block against the pressure of the explosion which was intended to thrust the projectile down the barrel. While the

charge – and therefore the projectile – was a small one this could be accomplished without any great difficulty. Many ingenious methods of holding the breech block against the pressure of a greater explosion were tried, often with fatal results. The early gunsmiths got within an ace of success with a screw thread in the breech block mating with a similar screw thread in the barrel. Large and effective siege guns were constructed on this principle. But the understanding of metallurgy and expansion coefficients was still very primitive. The explosion of one great charge made the gun so hot that it was many hours before the breech could be unscrewed. Guns like these on shipboard would clearly be limited to one shot in any action. Centuries were to pass before someone chanced on the clever ruse of using an in-

um preuilegio

LEFT: '*Northern carrack
and galley*', by Breughel

OPPOSITE: '*The destruction
of Spanish galleys*' by Jacob
van Heemskerk after the
Battle of Gibraltar, 1607.
The galley slaves are clearly
shown. They usually sank
with the galley, as it was
not safe to unchain them
from their benches

OVERLEAF (*left*): *The*
Great Harry, 1546, *pride
of Henry VIII's Navy, from
the Anthony Anthony Rolls.
Woolwich Dockyard grew
around her building; this
picture shows her after her
complete rebuild. The* Great
Harry, *the* Henry Grace à
Dieu *(1514, rebuilt between
1536 and 1539) and the* Mary
Rose *(1509) are the three
best-known vessels built by
Henry VIII*

OVERLEAF (*right*): *Two
details from 'Battle in the
Gulf of Naples', by Breughel*

BELOW: *The Turkish gun
at the Tower of London*

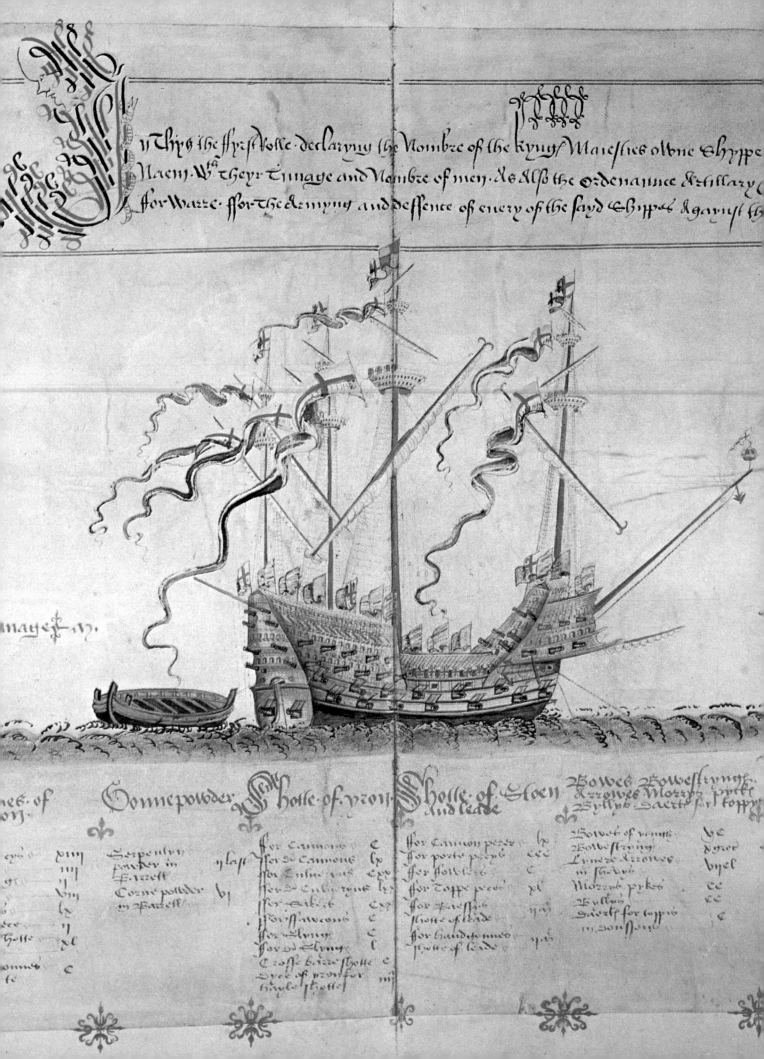

In Thys the ffyrst Rolle declaryng the Nombre of the kyngs Maiesties olde Shyppe Naem, wth theyr Tunnage and Nombre of men. As Alsso the ordenaunce Artillary for Warre. ffor the Armyng and deffence of every of the sayd Shyppes Agaynst th...

	Gonnepowder	Shotte of yron	Shotte of Ston and leade	Bowes, Bowestryngs, Arrowes, Morys pyke, Byllys, Dartts for toppys
	Serpentyn powder in Barrell	for Cannons	for Cannon perd	Bowes of yewgh
	Corne powder in Barrell	for gret Cannons	for porte pecys	Bowestrynggs
		ffor Culveryns	ffor Sloers	Lyvere Arrowes in Sheyffs
		ffor gret Culveryns	ffor Toppe pecys	Morys pykes
		ffor Sakers	for Fawcons	Byllys
		ffor Fawcons	Shotte of leade	Dartts for toppys in Dossyns
		ffor Slyngs	ffor handgonnes	
		ffor gret Slyngs	Shotte of leade	
		Crosse barre shotte		
		Dyse of yron for hayle shotte		

terrupted thread – the thread in the barrel and the breech block being broken by corresponding regular gaps – so that the block could be swung in and secured with one small twist. Instead, the early gunsmith was forced to take a step backwards and resort again to the single-piece gun – the muzzle-loader, which was to endure into the mid-1800s.

The cast muzzle-loader first began to supplement the light, built-up, breech-loading man-destroyer on shipboard in the early 1500s. The heathen Turk taught the Western Christian a lot about casting, and the evidence can be seen in the enormous Dardanelles Gun at the Tower of London. It is recorded that guns of this size (nearly 20 tons and almost unmoveable) were cast *in situ*, probably facing some troublesome wall. The material of these early cast guns was loosely termed 'brass', a compound at that time of 100 parts of copper, 10 parts of copper and zinc, and 8 parts of tin. The gun which was manufactured from cast iron came later.

The casting of guns in one piece was a retrograde step because loading them from the muzzle was a clumsy business. But they were much safer for the ship, and especially for the gunner who lit the fuse. The trunnions securing the gun to its mounting, and later even the ring for the breech-rope to hold the recoil, were all cast in one piece.

OPPOSITE: *An engraving of the* Henry Grace à Dieu *of 1514. It is interesting to compare this eighteenth-century reconstruction with Anthony Anthony's drawing on page 36*

BELOW: *The French fleet attacking Portsmouth in 1545, engraved by Basire*

The best-known, if not the first, Western gun-founder to perfect an effective cast brass big gun was Hans Poppenruyter of Malines. The art rapidly spread throughout Europe. There was no more enthusiastic advocate than Henry VIII, and in the early years of his reign he was encouraging English gun-founders to cast brass cannon and his shipwrights to install them in his new great fighting ships. During the later years of Henry's reign these were the chief weapons in common use in his navy:

Cannon The heaviest piece of artillery throwing an iron shot weighing about 50 pounds, the ultimate ship destroyer. Length of bore about 20 calibres. Maximum range about a mile.

Demi-cannon A similar cast piece throwing a 32-pound shot.

Culverin A very long and efficient piece much favoured in the English Navy. Weight of shot about 18 pounds, length 32 calibres. Maximum range about $1\frac{1}{4}$ miles.

Demi-culverin Similar, but with weight of ball half of the Culverin.

Saker, Minion, Falcon, Falconet and *Robinet* These were all smaller pieces designed to throw shot weighing from around 5 pounds to less than one pound. This smaller shot was lethal to both man and rigging at close quarters.

OVERLEAF *(left)*: *Two illustrations from Matthew Baker's 'Fragments of Ancient Shipwrightry' showing his design for a ship, and a master shipwright with a compass*

OVERLEAF *(right)*: *Detail of 'Portuguese carracks off a rocky coast', 1521, by Anthoniszoon*

The Spanish Armada : the Importance of Matériel

Spain, the mightiest naval and colonial power in the world, was defeated in 1588 because it continued, long after it should have done, to treat sea warfare as an extension of land warfare, with the infantryman as the first weapon, and man rather than his ship as the first target. Also Spanish men-of-war were inferior to those of the enemy in the waters on which they fought. Spain had created her vast empire largely through her maritime power and prowess. But the fighting had been conducted on land, by the best foot soldiers of their time. Spain's last massive and decisive victory at sea, at Lepanto, had similarly been achieved by the infantryman in close combat. It therefore seemed eminently reasonable that the Great Armada should number 19,000 soldiers and only 8,000 sailors; after all, England itself had to be conquered when the fleet had been dealt with. By contrast, the English flagship carried 270 seamen and 34 gunners, and only 126 soldiers to cope with the enemy soldiers in the unfortunate event of a boarding. The Spanish tactics were to pound the enemy ship with heavy short-range cannon, bear down on her while pouring from her fighting tops and high bulwarks and castles a rain of man-destroying projectiles, and then board with a fierce, self-confident body of men armed with pikes and swords. If everything worked out like this, the Spaniards were unbeatable. But in an era when the gunsmith could provide the fighting seaman with the means to destroy his enemy ship at a range of several hundred

yards, the boarding and capturing of ships was great sport but tactically obsolete. It also required speed and handiness superior to the enemy's.

Since the spring of 1586, when the Marquis of Santa Cruz had submitted to King Philip II of Spain his plan for the invasion of England, preparations had been going ahead for the construction and collection of the Great Armada.

Hakluyt tells us: 'The king Catholique had given commandment long before in Italy and Spaine, that a great quantitie of timber should be felled for the building of shippes; and had besides made great preparation of things and furniture requisite for such an expedition.' The 'king Catholique' was also misguided enough to order the inclusion of four Mediterranean galleys, all of which were forced back at the first meeting with rough weather; and four galleasses 'of such bignesse', Hakluyt reported, 'that they contained within them chambers, chapels, turrets, pulpits, and other commodities of great houses' together with 300 slave oarsmen each. There was rather more sense in the inclusion of these, the most spectacular and intimidating fighting ships of their day and with a really formidable armament, because, while they did little damage, they succeeded in engaging the anxious attention of the English for much of the way up-Channel.

To get the Armada fighting into perspective, several neat legends, stemming from contemporary English poets, the writings of G. A. Henty and even

quite recent history primers, have to be disposed of. A number of Medina Sidonia's galleons, while not vast floating castles, were of an impressive stature – which made them all the more difficult to handle. But most of them were merchantmen converted to troopships and carrying only a modest armament of cannon. The English commander, Charles, Lord Howard of Effingham, could muster no converted merchantman to match Sidonia's *La Ragonza*. But neither was his new galleon, *Triumph*, of 1,100 tons, matched in tonnage or power by any warship in the Spanish fleet.

Medina Sidonia's fleet for 'the enterprize of England' consisted of seventy-seven first-line ships, divided into six squadrons, or armadas, supported by forty-five storeships and smaller craft, the four galleys and the four Neapolitan galleasses. Of the main fighting force, around seven of the ships were of 1,000 tons or more, twice this number were between 800 and 1,000 tons, and the rest averaged about 400 tons. But of these only some twenty had been designed as fighting ships from the keel up; the remainder were tubby merchantmen mainly of carrack form, which had received an addition to their

standard armament. Santa Cruz, the victor at Lepanto seventeen years earlier, favoured the heavy cannon, and the main artillery power of the Armada lay in cannon and demi-cannon with a short barrel and capable of firing, over a very limited range, a round shot of 60 or 30 pounds. In total weight of broadside, the English could not match the Spaniards. But the long-barrel English culverin and demi-culverin far outranged the Spanish guns. The situation was analogous to a heavyweight boxer with a short reach and a pulverizing punch challenging a flyweight with a long reach. With the English Channel as the ring, all else being equal it would seem to be only a matter of time before the heavyweight triumphed. But the flyweight had a further and overwhelming advantage: he was very much quicker on his feet, and his reflexes were twice as fast. For the only time in Britain's long maritime history, the Navy's *matériel* was the finest in the world.

The Queen's ships built under the administration of Howard as Lord High Admiral were not in any way revolutionary. Rather, they represented a natural and inevitable trend in fighting ship design, impelled by the growing efficiency and ship-destroying power of contemporary ordnance, which other nations – even the Dutch – were slower to accept. For the first time in the history of warship design, there is detailed documentary evidence of measurements and plans of the vessels. Matthew Baker, the first Master Shipwright appointed by the Crown, left a manuscript (now in the Pepysian Library at Magdalene College, Cambridge) containing elevations, plans and sections of several ships. It is evident from these

BELOW *(left)*: The Ark Royal, *Howard's flagship against the Armada*

BELOW *(centre)*: *Visscher's idea of the same ship*

BELOW *(right)*: *Matthew Baker's design for a ship of the time of the Armada*

OVERLEAF: *'The Battle' by Vroom which shows the Spanish Armada of 1588*

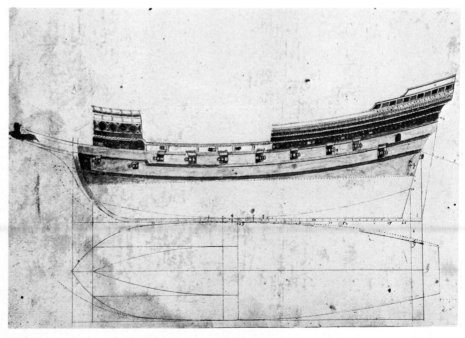

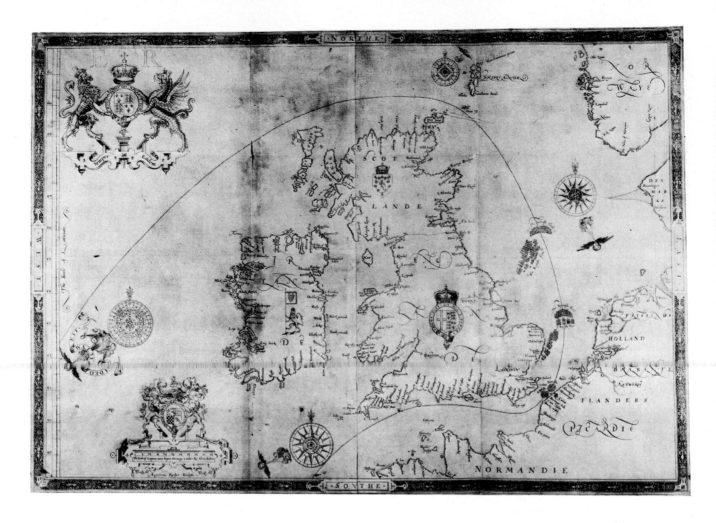

documents, and from a list of 1600, that the English fighting ship which defeated the Armada had a keel length at least three times its breadth; had a forecastle set well back from the stem and a projecting beak; a strong sheer, or upward curve of the hull towards both stern and bow; and transom, or square, stern. The old extravagance of built-up castles fore and aft had now quite disappeared; instead, by successive stages aft of the mainmast there arose half deck, quarter deck and poop. The rig was four-masted in ten of Howard's ships, most of the others carrying fore, main and mizzen only.

The main armament of culverins and demi-culverins was arranged on the broadside at several different levels because it was an invariable rule that the wales, on which the longitudinal strength of the ship depended, must not be pierced. Because of the ship's steep sheer the gunports rose by stages forward and aft from the waist. The lighter guns were carried in the forecastle and the half deck, in the waist, and in the beakhead bulkhead, which provided forward fire which was effective against men and rigging.

This was the type of English galleon which formed the most formidable attacking weight of the English fleet. The English captains were proud of them and loved them. Gifted with native skill as well as experience in seamanship, burning with zeal and a fierce hatred of the Catholic invader, with ships such as these as well as all the natural advantages enjoyed by a defending fleet close to its supplies and reinforcements, could Howard and his commanders fail?

They could have failed for several reasons. First, only a handful of the English fighting ships were of the latest swift and powerful class. While no fewer than 197 vessels are listed as taking part in the attacks, the vast majority of these were small merchantmen, pinnaces and fishing vessels of negligible fighting value compared with the *Ark Royal* with her 44 guns. Only fourteen of Howard's ships were of more than 500 tons, and the decisive fighting which decided the fate of England and of Medina Sidonia's Armada was conducted by no more than some twenty ships on each side. Second, the Spanish fought

46

with skill and tenacity, and their formation, in a loose crescent or triangle with the most powerful ships in the centre protecting the supply ships ahead, proved to be almost unbreakable. Finally, Howard's crippling handicap was a simple logistical miscalculation of the expected expenditure of powder and shot required for the harassing attacks by the English ships all the way up the Channel.

In spite of the courage of the foe and the recurrent shortage of ammunition, the English galleons swept in time and again to a range just beyond that of the heavier Spanish guns and fired their broadsides of culverins and demi-culverins. Many of their shots damaged the Spanish rigging and plunged into the upper works to spread deadly wooden splinters among those exposed on deck. But most of them were delivered 'on the downward roll' of the ship so that the shots struck low on the stout sides of the Spanish ships: each broadside a shattering confirmation of the English determination to destroy the ship. In fact the structural damage from a culverin ball was comparatively slight; and the vast Spanish fleet sailed implacably on, and questions were asked by the Queen's Council why none of the perfidious Catholic ships had yet been boarded. This was just what Medina Sidónia was praying for – and he could do little more under the circumstances. He had been warned that there was little likelihood of good, old-fashioned, man-to-man combat: 'The enemy will fight at long range to get the advantage of his artillery,' King Philip had told him. But it was impossible for Medina Sidonia to follow his orders that he 'must close and grapple, taking them in your hand' when the English could beat back into the wind almost before the Spanish steersman could put over the helm. At the time it was necessary to defend Howard's tactics against ignorant criticism, while the fate of England still hung on the effective handling of a few hundred pieces of light artillery against ships containing 19,000 eager but frustrated Spanish foot soldiers.

Besides being one of the most decisive sea battles

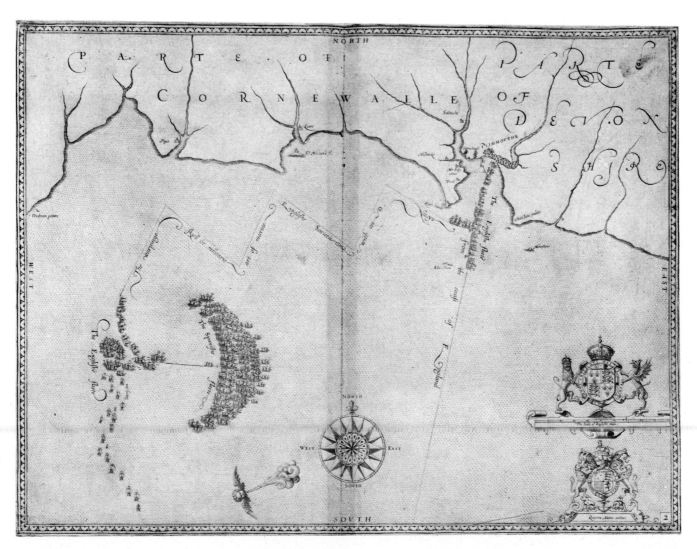

of all time, the defeat of the Spanish Armada marks the beginning of naval warfare in a form and tradition that was to endure until the aircraft took over the rôle of the cannon 350 years later. The English ships triumphed because they presaged the age of the line-of-battle and were the first battleships to take part in a major and decisive conflict. The Spanish galleons were defeated as decisively as the battleships were later defeated at Taranto and Pearl Harbor, because they remained armed troopships when the new battleship with longer-ranging artillery was manifestly the new queen of the sea; just as the steel battleship itself was defeated in the 1940s because it was vulnerable to the new longer-ranging artillery of the aircraft carrier – the bomb and the torpedo.

The Spanish defeat marked the opening of the new age of sea warfare when the *matériel* – beyond the cutlass, the pike and the sword – began to dominate sea warfare. The quality of the personnel, goodness knows, was to continue to count in the statistical results of battle and gallant combats against great odds were to touch with gold the annals of sea warfare for centuries to come. But the modern fighting ship was born, the age of dominance of the *matériel* began, when Charles Lord Howard, soon after 9 am on the morning of Sunday 31 July 1588, bore down in the *Ark Royal* on Don Alfonso de Leiva's great galleon the *Rata Coronada* and poured into her ample hull a broadside of 9-pounder and 18-pounder round shot. At 3.47 pm on the afternoon of 31 May 1916, Vice-Admiral Sir David Beatty opened fire on the German battle cruisers and began the last great combat between artillery-armed fighting ships. In the intervening years the fighting ship was to suffer many changes in its size and shape, motive power and gun power. The basic principles and conduct of maritime warfare changed not at all

OPPOSITE *(above)*: *'After the Battle' by Vroom*

OPPOSITE *(below)*: *Portrait of Queen Elizabeth I with two scenes of the Spanish Armada behind her*

BELOW: *One of Pine's tapestry hanging designs of the Armada*

Dutch and French Superiority

The seventeenth century marked a period of powerful colonial rivalry and conflict, in which the chief contestants were France, Holland, England and Spain. There had been frequent and fundamental changes in the shape of the fighting ship following the introduction of the third mast and the ship-destroying gun in the 1400s and 1500s. There remained to the architect plenty of opportunity for radical improvement of his ships in the succeeding decades, but none that were to alter greatly the form. This was a century of consolidation rather than evolution. The most dogged, sagacious and successful colonists of this century were the Dutch. Dutch colonialism and affluence were brought about by a series of historical events, one of the most important being the defeat at sea of Spain by England in 1588. But long before then the Dutch had begun to struggle free from the Hapsburg spider's web. The sea and their heroic physical struggle against it, their native acumen and acquisitiveness, had for long made the Dutch acutely maritime-conscious. In the late 1500s they were building armed galleons that could sail far beyond their native shores to bring back home the riches of the East Indies – without the advantage

of a call en route at Lisbon, closed to them as a result of their own rebellion. Good fortune assisted their courage and endeavours. The shrewd Queen of England, who had struck such a blow at their oppressors, died at last in 1603, and a king who misguidedly over-prized peace ascended the throne. The English Navy decayed while Dutch sea power soared higher and higher in unison with the wealth of the merchants of Rotterdam and Amsterdam.

The Dutch warships of the mid-1600s were smaller and less heavily armed than the largest English ships. The need to restrict their draught, because of the sandbanks of the Dutch coast, limited them to two gun decks, although by judicious use of the space eighty and even ninety guns were sometimes carried. By skilful formation of the hull and a shrewd understanding of sails and rigging and the sailing qualities of a ship, their vessels were both swifter and more manoeuvrable than their English counterparts, although these advantages were probably entirely wiped out when fighting in the open sea. The biggest vessels were three-masters, with a much reduced sheer compared with the galleons of the last century. The forecastle had almost ceased to exist, the beak-

ABOVE: '*The Four Days' Fight*', *1666, by Storck. This was the first time, except for isolated occasions such as the Armada, that regular fleets of over 100 sail a side engaged in mortal combat with one another – the name of the battle is indicative. On the right is the English ship with the royal arms, left, is the Dutch ship with her state arms on the tafferel*

OPPOSITE: '*The Battle of Ter Heide*', *1653, by Beerstraten. This is a typical contemporary version of a sea battle*

head thrust upwards more markedly, the stern – in contrast with latest English practice – was square. Dutch naval architects were the first to recognize the extreme and wasteful degree to which the tumble-home had developed, and sought by more scientific means to offset the imbalance caused by many heavy cannon above the centre of gravity. Other nations conformed to Dutch straight-sided practice, but not until much later. The Dutch gained further speed by tallowing the bottoms of their ships against barnacles, and here again they were first. Dutch skill with sails resulted in their introduction of the first modern fore and aft rig, which was widely used in their highly admired *jachts*. At the other end of the scale, the Dutch led the world, too, with their fire-

ships – the torpedoes of the 1600s – which Dutch flagships had under their lee ready to be despatched at suitable moments in battle: one of these being at Solebay when the English flagship *Royal James* was set on fire and destroyed.

The superiority of Dutch shipbuilding before and during the Anglo-Dutch wars was widely recognized in Europe. The Swedes, the Danes and the Germans all took advantage of Dutch wisdom. Peter the Great of Russia came to Zaandam in 1667 to make a personal study of Dutch methods. The origins and inspiration of one of the other great navies in Europe can be traced back to Holland in the 1620s, long before Dutch colonial power had reached its zenith. In 1624 France possessed almost no power at sea. Richelieu, who came to office in that year, recognized this desperate weakness. With no tradition of modern fighting ship construction to draw on, he turned to the best and most experienced builders. Five large ships with sixty guns disposed on two decks, and with the most up-to-date sail and rigging, were ordered from the Dutch yards. They were an immediate success, and French shipwrights were ordered to study

51

BELOW: *A Louis XIV first rate. In Louis XIV's reign Colbert, the Minister of Marine, was very interested in the growth and improvement of the Navy, and today a number of beautiful manuscripts, prepared for presentation to the King, survive with admirable pictures of different rates of ships. This is a first rate ship of about 100 guns, and such a ship, after suitable prepara-tion, could be put together by Colbert's well-organized dockyards in a remarkably short time. Colbert set up arsenals, a gunnery school and the great dockyards of Toulon and Brest. This intensive injection of maritime enthusiasm resulted in Louis XIV possessing before his death the most advanced and efficient fighting fleet in Europe*

them. They learnt their lessons well. The 72-gun two-decker *Couronne* of 1638 was a very fine sailer and by her very dexterity (in turning to present her other broadside) could probably fire as many guns in any given period as a contemporary British 100-gun ship.

In their turn, other maritime powers made a closer and more scientific study of naval architecture during the 1600s, and benefited greatly from Dutch, French and English practice. Among these was Sweden, which built up a formidable navy in the early part of the century. Fortunately, in this case we have the unique advantage of an actual ship to study. The foundering of the Dutch-designed *Wasa* off Beckholmen on her maiden voyage in 1628 was a major catastrophe for the Swedish people; her location, and her subsequent salvaging between 1959 and 1961 was a major feat.

The English navy began the new century in fine fettle. The golden glow of triumph from the victory of 1588 still lingered over the fleet and the men who had sailed out to meet Medina Sidonia; but the sun-

LEFT: *A reconstruction of the* Wasa, *by Stodberg. The* Wasa *sank in Stockholm harbour on her maiden voyage. Plans for her reconstruction are going forward and much has been learned since this picture was produced*

BELOW: *The* Wasa *in dry dock. She was raised in 1961 after lying on the sea bed for 333 years. The* Wasa *museum contains the almost complete hull of the seventeenth-century warship in pristine condition, and also guns, gear, equipment and even the personal effects of the officers and crew*

set was near, and soon after the accession of King James I in 1603 the Navy, through neglect and absence of funds, slipped into a decline. This idealistic King even tried to stamp out free-lance English piracy, an activity which had not only filled the nation's coffers but also taught the men who fought the Armada skilful seamanship and fighting prowess. In 1607 the Venetian ambassador in London reported home that even the few serviceable fighting ships left were 'old and rotten and barely fit for service'. As a result of this misguided policy, piracy by others flourished around England's shores, trade declined, and the new colonial powers – who had drawn their own more accurate conclusions from Spain's defeat at sea – were encouraged to build up new navies.

Fortunately, the slump was only temporary. With the restoration of the English monarchy in 1660 there begins a period of renewed naval enthusiasm and construction. The continuing competition from Holland, the ever-growing power of France and a wave of popular interest in all things naval – comparable with the closing years of Victoria's reign 200 years later – which was inspired and nourished by King Charles II, all led to a splendid renaissance.

European naval competition in the second half of the century produced a shortage of skilled men and materials comparable with that of the years before the First World War. Timber was imported in great quantities from the Baltic, and it was not so satisfactory or long-lasting as home-grown oak. England, with her great reserves of finest standing oak, was at an advantage. But even before Charles II's Act of 1677, calling for thirty new men-of-war, unprecedented demand on the oak reserves of the Royal forests, and wilful neglect to replant in the past, led to the need to import. Imported elm and beech for the keel and lower planking of English ships proved unsatisfactory and deteriorated rapidly. Under the stress of this shortage, iron was used for certain internal fittings. Nails, standards and knees of iron became more and more widely used, even in the English Navy, to the distress of Samuel Pepys, famous diarist and secretary to the Admiralty, who considered the departure 'most unfavourable'.

RIGHT: *Rigging plans of a fourth and (far right) a sixth rate ship from 'Doctrine of Naval Architecture', by Sir Antony Deane*

OPPOSITE *(below)*: *The* Sovereign of the Seas, *1637, from a contemporary engraving by Payne. She was the great ship of Charles I's Navy, the first with three masts instead of the usual four (see the* Prince Royal), *and had royals on the main and foremast, topgallants on all three masts. She was highly decorated and became known as 'The Golden Devil', though she was only in action once. Samuel Pepys and a large number of his friends were able to get inside the poop lantern, which gives an indication of her enormous size*

BELOW: *The* Prince Royal, *1610, at Flushing. The harbour could be recognized today*

55

Ship Decoration

During the 1600s the embellishment of the fighting ship by carving, gilding and painting was practised enthusiastically and skilfully by all the European sea powers, from the Venetians and Genoese in the south to the Danes and Swedes in the north. In a century of dazzling splendour everywhere, the ships of Louis XIV just outshone the strong competition. Looking at the contemporary model of the English first rate H.M.S. *Prince*, it is hard to conceive that a stern could be more elaborately carved. But the great French decorator Pierre Pugin had no peer and could out-embellish the greatest carvers of his day with his pilaster work, his figure carving, his heavy balustrading for galleries, his arches and canopies over a ship's entering ports, his life-size figures on a ship's hancing pieces – the step made by the drop of a ship's rail to another level. Such was the ostentation of decoration of French men-of-war that captains were reduced to disguising them with canvas sheets in an endeavour

to persuade pirate captains that they were only merchantmen. An even more graphic scene is presented by another old salt sawing off, in fury and exasperation, the great stern figures which added dangerous top weight to his vessel, and letting them fall overboard. It is fair to add, however, that the great majority of mariners accepted this burden of embellishment as no more than a further hazard to the whole dangerous business of life at sea. Thus were the fruits of the artist dealt with by the man of action.

The stern offered the greatest opportunity for the decorator. The introduction of windows, galleries and gunports provided the justification for further elaboration. The practical French Minister of Marine, Colbert, protested in vain against the vulgar and expensive practice of overloading by over-carving.

The Dutch, as befitted their business-like temperament, restrained the enthusiasm of their carvers and gilders more successfully than the French or English, and early showed their good sense by exhibiting paintings by contemporary artists. The sides of their two-deckers were quite plain and business-

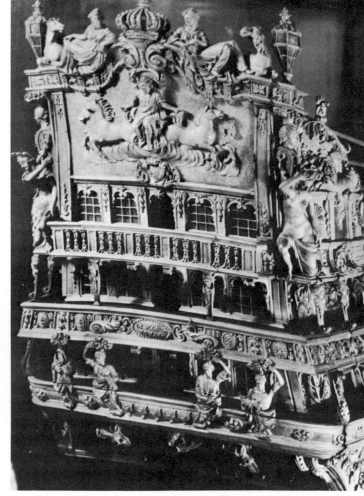

like. The figurehead was normally a fierce but simple red-painted lion; only at the stern was there any lavishness in the treatment of carving, gilding and painting.

The English began the century in a sober frame of mind, the decorations of their men-of-war reflecting the contemporary Tudor-Gothic style of interior decoration ashore. The effects of the Renaissance took a while to cross the Channel; but soon, in the *Prince Royal*, the English had the most decorated – as well as the largest – warship in the world. The upper two of her three stern galleries were illuminated by rows of windows, and the coat-of-arms of the Prince of Wales had the plumes painted white against the surrounding gilding and background green painting (cost: £868 6s 8d). But this fighting ship was a Plain Jane alongside the *Sovereign of the Seas*, of which Phineas Pett despairingly wrote in his journals that 'she was so gorgeously ornamented with carving and gilding, that she seemed to have been designed rather for a vain display of magnificence than for the services of the state'.

RIGHT: *Drawing by Van de Velde of the ornamentation on the stern of the* Royal Charles

OPPOSITE: *Ornamentation on models of the* Soleil Royal *(right) and the* Louis Quinze *(left). This magnificent flagship of Louis XV's Navy was burnt by the English at Cape La Hogue, 1692, under the eyes of Marshal Turin and the exiled James II*

BELOW: *A later style of ornamentation designed for a French eighteenth-century frigate by Ozanne. The French seventeenth- and eighteenth-century figurehead was larger and heavier than its English equivalent*

Sail and Rig in the 1600s

There was little development in sails and rigging in the first part of the century. A typical Dutch-built three-masted galleon of the 1620s already carried a topsail on the sprit topmast above the bowsprit as well as spritsail below. Fore and mainsail were furled with buntlines, clewlines and martnets; and topgallantsails were carried above the fore and mainmasts, but there were only two sails, square sail above a lateen, on the mizzen, with martnet and lift for furling. The *Sovereign of the Seas* designed a decade later sported a remarkably elaborate plan with no less than thirteen sails, although it is likely that the two royals were only for show. The main weakness of the sail arrangement in the 1600s – as it had been for centuries – was in the headsails. The spritsail topsail was, to the eye as well as in practice, a clumsy and inefficient makeshift, and it could not be long before the implacable conservatism of the seamen was at last overcome. As so often with 'new' inventions it was only necessary for the innovator to look backwards in time; for the canny Dutch had worked everything out in their sloops of a century earlier with their triangular-shaped headsail, or jib, stayed between the foremast and bowsprit. It was the Dutch who led the way again, adopting this same practice for their big ships, while retaining the spritsail be-

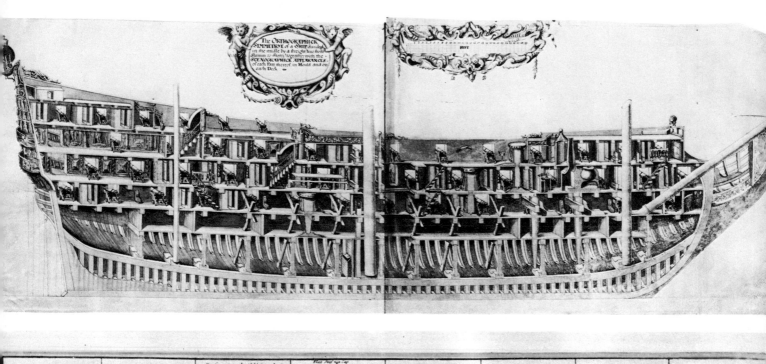

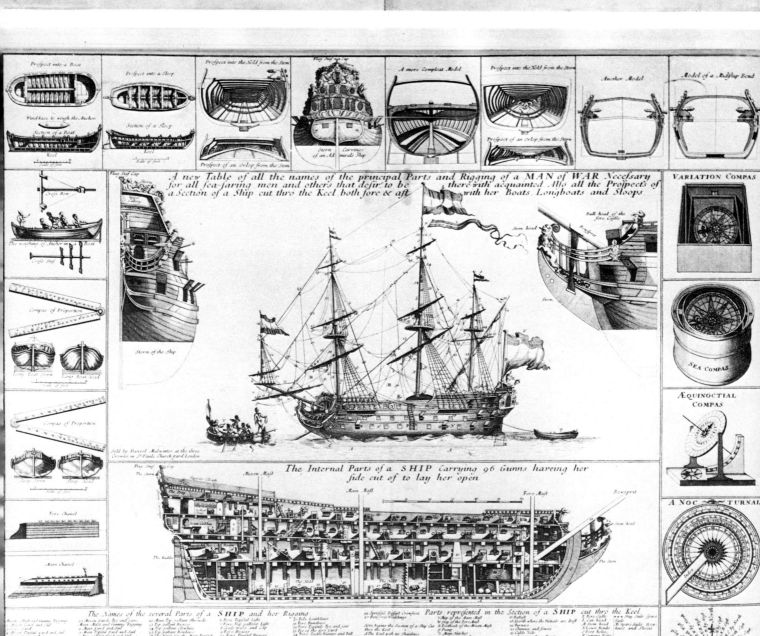

neath the bowsprit. The introduction of triangular headsails, which permitted dramatically more efficient sailing to windward, was the first really radical departure in sails since the introduction of the spritsail. Its long-term results were much more profound. In the early years of the next century, it led to the adoption everywhere of main and foretopmast staysails, and also to the use of studding sails which again were not new but whose qualities had not before been fully explored. The wide acceptance of the jib led to the melting away of many of the mariners' prejudices against sail innovation, so that within a few decades from the end of the 1600s the science of rigging and sails had advanced rapidly.

A further notable advance in sail arrangements during the 1600s was in the method of reducing sail. For many years sail had been reduced by tying up at a line of reef points either at the top or bottom of the sail. With the introduction of the three-masted-ship, bonnets were introduced. These were an additional depth of sail laced to the foot of the course, which could quickly be taken off. But the bonnet could not be used on the smaller topsails, which could only be furled when the yard was lowered. This be-

came a more and more formidable undertaking with the increase in size of the upper sails, and reef points had therefore to be added to these sails too, their number increasing with the size of the sail.

Underwater Protection

The protection of a ship's bottom from corrosion and rot and the depredations of barnacles and worms and seaweed had been an occasional anxiety even on the shorter voyages in the ancient world. With the lengthening of voyages to many weeks and the tactical need to stay at sea, later perhaps for blockading purposes, it became necessary to give more serious attention to the problem, especially in ships sailing in tropical waters, where the ravages of the teredo were so dangerous. In the 1500s Hawkins had thought up the idea of covering the outside of the planking with a composition of felt, hair and tar, nailing over it a sheathing of elm boards. This was a brave shot in the right direction but it did not work very well, and like a gold cap to a tooth, the decay went on beneath until the timbers at length fell apart. Lead sheathing was tried later in the 1600s, but electrolytic action caused the nails to fall out and it was very heavy. Copper sheathing was the answer, though of course it was very expensive and at first it only accelerated the corrosion of the iron bolts of the hull behind the copper. In the late 1700s copper bolts replaced these iron bolts, and all was well.

OPPOSITE (above): A section of a third rate warship from Mr Dummer's 'Draughts of the Body of an English Man of War'

OPPOSITE (below): Table of all the 'principal parts and rigging' of a Dutch man-of-war. This was the epitome of Dutch shipping at the end of the seventeenth century

LEFT: A model of a 60-gun ship of 1715 showing the influence of Chinoiserie in its decoration

A Century of Conflict

The eighteenth century was the last full century in the life of the sailing warship. Again the one hundred years witnessed a steady and unspectacular development in all branches of naval science. In its hull formation, masting, sail plan and the disposition of its armament the sailing warship closely approached a degree of efficiency beyond which no further progress could be made. Before the century was out the first experiments were being conducted with mechanical in place of natural power for the ship, and a few farsighted and courageous artillery enthusiasts were demonstrating the fearful effects of explosive against the structure of the wooden ship.

There was much fighting at sea during this century, mainly among the French, Spanish and English, and towards the end, the Americans too. The Anglo-French wars added lustre to the naval records of both countries. The British suffered many setbacks and defeats but proved themselves the more skilful fight-

ers. Their ships were the least felicitous and effective in design. 'To sum up the character of the English vessels of this period [early 1700s],' wrote John Charnock, the notable naval historian, 100 years later, 'in general terms, they were crank, confined, very indifferently adapted to the purposes of keeping out the sea in tempestuous weather, and in general but sorry sailers, even when it was most favourable.'

In spite of the stalwart endeavours of some individuals and well-intentioned official attempts to get to grips with the shortcomings of British ship design, the application of science and the experience of the men who sailed them somehow escaped the naval architects of this great maritime nation until the very end of the century. The French naval engineer possessed the priceless ability to step back and judge problems with his characteristic engineering originality, fresh and unprejudiced by tradition for its own sake. Craftsmanship by eye was a deeply ingrained English tradition. In the time of James I, Captain George Waymouth, an advanced shipbuilding theorist, complained that he 'could never see two

ships builded of the like proportion by the best and most skilful shipwrights, though they have many times undertaken the same...because they trust rather to their judgement than their art, and to their eye than their scale and compass.'

The Spaniards were never able to make up for the deficiencies of their fighting seamen. But they built some of the best fighting ships of the century by recognizing the special qualities of their friends and their enemies – by importing French engineers to design them and British master shipwrights to construct them. Such giants of the mid-1700s as the 114-gun *Real Infanta*, or the 70-gun *Isabella*, *Hercule* and *Constant*, were unsurpassed even by any French fighting ship. The British kept no more than one step behind by capturing, thanks to superior seaman-

ship, both French and Spanish ships and copying them. Time and again the canny sailing skill of the British was rendered impotent by the superior sailing qualities of French and Spanish ships – for science had been at work on the shape of their hulls and the arrangement of their sails.

With the firm establishment in the 1600s of the distinction of the fighting ship from the merchantman, and the great increase in numbers and complexity of the fighting fleet, it had become necessary for all navies to classify their vessels in various categories. A system of 'rating' according to the number of guns had been accepted by the English Navy in the middle of that century, thus:

First rate	100 guns
Second rate	52 guns
Third rate	46 guns
Fourth rate	40 guns
Fifth rate	24 guns
Sixth rate	18 guns

With the inevitable increase in the size of ship brought about by the Dutch wars the rating require-

OPPOSITE: *Admiral de Winter at Camperdown with the* Monarch, Ardent *and* Venerable, *by Serres*

BELOW: '*The Battle of Gibraltar*', *1607, by Vroom. The explosion is probably the powder magazine of the Spanish ship igniting and blowing up*

ment was raised for all but the sixth rates. It was generally accepted that the first four rates were fit to lie in the line of battle, but there was a great deal of confusion about this, and much else too, until the administration of Anson. Anson was the Lord Fisher of the 1700s; without his clarity of vision and enterprise and energy the victories at sea against the French at the end of the century would never have happened. Besides introducing some measure of standardization into ship construction (not much perhaps, but it was a start), he laid down that nothing under 64-gun ships should stand in the line of battle. Later in the century and during the Napoleonic wars the British line-of-battle was even more neatly made up from two-gundecked 74s and flagships of 100 guns or more. Although the sailing quality of the individual ships in these two categories varied widely, for strict uniformity in ship construction was still a hundred years away, this near-homogeneity added immeasurably to the power and control of the line-of-battle.

The shape of the ship-of-the-line changed, but not very markedly, during the century. The most noticeable difference between, say, the *Prince* of 1670 and the *Victory* built just 105 years later was the absence of rake, which had been steadily diminishing over the years since the acute almost hoop-like form of the carracks of the 1400s.

The forward castle had quite disappeared by the mid-1700s, and survived in name alone, as the forecastle deck, raised from the waist of the ship, and growing longer decade by decade. The aftercastle, too, had gone, even to its name. Its vestigial remnants were the quarter deck, raised above the main deck just abaft of midships, and above it again the poop, under the break of which the ship was still steered – no longer by the whipstaff but by a wheel, except in smaller ships, from the early years of the century. A glance at the bows helped to confirm the distinction between a large fighting ship, whether Spanish, French or British, of the late 1700s from the late 1600s.

The head had become progressively deeper and shorter and, starting with the smaller vessels, then began to disappear altogether so that the bow reverted to a shape more closely resembling the old rounded form. This had the twin advantages of keeping the ship much drier in a head sea and allowing for an increase in the number of guns that could be brought to bear on either bow. The reshaping of the stern became evident, too, during the 1700s. Although the stern-walk had made its first appearance in English ships in the late 1600s, some years passed

ABOVE: '*The Battle of the Nile' (detail)*, 1798, by Pocock. *This was painted to be engraved as an illustration to Clarke and McArthur's 'Life of Nelson', produced in 1816*

OPPOSITE: *Model of a carronade in the Musée de la Marine, Paris*

before it began to project beyond the stern. The single stern-walk of the two-deckers was doubled up in three-deckers normally, but there was no hard-and-fast rule about this.

By the end of the 1700s the fighting ship was almost fully matured in its sails and rigging. Every stay had its own staysail, and there was a jib set on the jib-boom, although the spritsail and spritsail topsail were sometimes retained as well, for no apparent good purpose except to please the traditionalists and provide the men with yet more exercise. These two redundant sails slowly disappeared after 1750, although they were still to be seen more than half a century later. With the exception of the royals, every sail on fore and main masts had its own pair of studding sails. There were important changes on the mizzen mast, too. The lower sail, or course, was greatly reduced in size until the whole sail lay abaft the mast, and the lateen yard developed, through a gaff, to a driver which projected over the stern and was set by a long boom. French ship design retained its ascendancy throughout the whole of the eighteenth century.

Gunnery Improvements

At the beginning of the eighteenth century the ship-of-the-line still carried everything from heavy ship-destroying cannon to man-destroying sakers, and the seaman with the musket high in the fighting tops was to continue to play an important rôle (including the killing of Lord Nelson) for another hundred years and more. Cannon became heavier, their recoil more powerful and violent, requiring ever bigger and heavier ships. When firing heavy shot, the cannon had a more or less accurate range of some 400 yards; but the hole it made in the enemy's timbers could, given resolution and speed, be plugged. Even a 42-pounder cannon firing at point-blank range might not pierce the two-feet-thick timber at the water line of some of the heaviest ships. It took a lot of firing to sink a big ship as a direct result of cannon fire. The most likely way of destroying the enemy was by the chance ignition of his powder, which was all over the gun decks and mainly unprotected. In spite of this very high explosion and fire risk, ships were still much more often captured than sunk.

The carronade was the most notable new weapon of the late 1700s. Its invention is attributed to General Robert Melville, and it was named after the River Carron near Falkirk in Scotland. Ironworks had been set up here because of the area's coal and iron deposits, and one of the largest was the Carron Company. The 'smasher' as the carronade came to be called was really an improved version of the old perrier – a stumpy-looking gun with a wide bore and a thin barrel designed to fire a hollow shot with great penetrating power over a short range. Its lightness was its great merit. The fighting sailor's demand for more and more big and heavy cannon in a vessel that was still swift and handy had set the naval architect an impossible task. The carronade helped greatly to solve the problem of compromise. The barrel itself was light, and this meant a light truck carriage, to which it was secured by lugs to a piece of timber which slid into the carriage. There were, therefore, no trunnions. The hollow shot called for a lighter charge, and thus less recoil. It was elevated by a screw fixed to the slide. The carronade was not only a most effective ship-destroyer; it was so light that it could be mounted high up in the ship, even on the poop or quarterdeck. Its one great drawback was its short range – a mere 100 yards. So a ship carrying only 'smashers' (and some did) could be smashed at long range by a well-handled ship carrying only cannon.

There were other drawbacks. 'Several captains complained of the carronade,' wrote William James in his *Naval History* of 1888. 'Some, of its upsetting after being heated by successive discharges; others, that, owing to its shortness, its fire scarcely passed clear of the ship's side.... The captains of some of

the 32-gun frigates, in particular, represented that one pair of the quarterdeck carronades was so much in the way of the rigging as to endanger the lanyards of the shrouds, and begged to have their established number reduced from six to four.'

The British carronade really came into its own and justified itself at the Battle of the Saints Passage in 1782. On this occasion the French were also surprised and savagely damaged by another British innovation. This was oblique fire, introduced into the service by Sir Charles Douglas. Douglas was the most inventive gunnery expert of the 1700s. He diminished the violence of recoil by combining ingenuity with simplicity: he put an inclined plane behind the rear wheels of the gun carriage and placed springs in the breeching. He also made things much safer for the gunners (though their job continued to be extremely hazardous for many years yet)

by suggesting that the charge could be safely ignited by a lanyard-pulled flintlock instead of a lighted match. The introduction of oblique fire was another of those seemingly obvious improvements in gunnery which make us wonder at the slow-wittedness of our ancestors. Until almost the end of the 1700s a ship's broadside could be fired to hit the enemy only when it bore close to 90 and 270 degrees – or at right-angles to the vessel's course. The act of traversing, thought up by Sir Charles Douglas, allowed each gun to be swung and fired 45 degrees before or abaft the beam. It astonished the French and revolutionized tactics by signalling the end of the formal set-piece battle with the opposing fleet sailing in strict line-ahead on parallel courses blasting off at one another as fast as the guns could be re-loaded. The oblique-firing gun helped to instil a new sense of freedom of operation in the conduct of sea battles.

ABOVE: *The Leeward Islands convoy being delivered by the* Portland *to the* Thames, *1776, by Luny. From early times, and particularly during the mid-seventeenth-century wars with the Dutch, it was customary to gather merchant ships into fleets to be convoyed through enemy-controlled waters, a practice revived in nineteenth- and twentieth-century conflicts*

ABOVE: *The* Sovereign of the Seas, *1637, anon. Peter Pett, on the right, was a master shipwright, and his masterpiece was built for Charles I at Woolwich. The bows were equally stun-* *ning, for the royal master carver, Gerard Christmas, worked from the drawings of the Dutch artist, Van Dyck, who gave special attention to the front*

The Frigate

From almost its earliest days the fighting ship has been supported by its minions, its messengers, its protectors, its scouts. The Mediterranean galley had its *fregata,* a close replica of itself in miniature, to act as a swift tender. In northern waters the term 'frigate' was first used in the 1500s to describe a small, sail-driven vessel, very like the galleons it served but narrower in proportion to its length. As naval fighting became more sophisticated, as it became increasingly possible for fleets to travel great distances and to remain at sea for longer periods, the need arose for small craft for scouting and communications. Hawkins had his scouts – his 'eyes' – to watch what was going on in Spain in 1587 and 1588. He had eighteen ocean-going pinnaces, and they did not miss a thing. When the Armada sailed, its daily progress, its distance from British shores, were both known. Thus it was quite possible for Drake, while awaiting its appearance, to play bowls calmly on Plymouth Hoe – although he did no such thing.

The classic frigate, the three-masted swift, single-gun-decked fighting ship – the type which Nelson would have had engraved on his heart for want of them, had he died in 1798 – did not make its appearance until the mid-1700s. In 1757, the year following the end of the Seven Years' War the British built, to the designs of Sir Thomas Slade, two single-gun-decked three-masted frigates, the *Pallas* and *Brilliant.* These frigates, and the French *Aurore* built at the same time, set the pattern for the genuine 36-gun frigates, which were to be built by the score for the French, Spanish, Dutch, British and American navies over the following fifty years, and were to serve so successfully in their multitudinous duties all over the world, convoying, scouting, patrolling, attacking and protecting commerce. The French and British built the most, and the French frigates were notably superior. Once again size and science counted. Look at these comparative figures for the *Aurore* and *Brilliant:*

	Tons	Keel	Beam	Guns
Brilliant	718	106'2$\frac{1}{2}$"	35'8"	36
Aurore	946	118'9"	38'8$\frac{1}{2}$"	36

A year later the British captured the *Aurore,* renamed her *Aurora,* admired her, took her measurements and learned many lessons from her.

Many different classes of frigate – from 40 to 20 guns – were built by the British during the second half of the century. Typical of her type was the *Minerva,* launched in 1780, the first of a new 38-gun class. When she joined the fleet she carried twenty eight 18-pounders on her main deck, and on her forecastle and quarterdeck ten 9-pounders and eight 18-pounder carronades, together with 14 swivel guns. At this time, over a period of some eight years, thirty 28-gun frigates were built. Representative of this class was the *Ariel,* of which there is a beautiful model in the Science Museum in London. Under the command of Captain Thomas Mackenzie she was pursued by the French frigate *Amazone* on 10 September 1779 and after an action lasting ninety minutes, during which she lost one of her masts and suffered twenty-four casualties, struck her colours.

The trim, elegant frigate of the late 1700s, like their counterparts and namesakes of the Second World War, were the workhorses of the French and British fleets and were in frequent action. Neither the French, Spanish, Dutch, Americans nor British ever had enough of them. The British navy possessed thirty-five in 1760. In 1798, when Nelson so deeply felt his lack of them, there were around a hundred in commission.

The Americans built the best frigates in the world – see page 82.

The Corvette and Other Small Vessels

The nomenclature of the various classes of fighting ship at different dates is almost impossible to sort out. Even the origin of some of the terms – let alone the ships they describe – is obscure. Does the word 'sloop' come from shallop, the rowed pinnace of the 1500s? Very likely it does. By the eighteenth century the British sloop – called a corvette in France – had grown up into a junior frigate, with perhaps eighteen guns on the upper deck. She was fully rigged, the sloop with three masts, the brig with two masts, but for a while oars might still be used as a last resort. By the end of the century a French corvette might be as formidable an antagonist as a British frigate, with three masts and guns on a gun deck – 12-pounders at that, instead of 6- or 9-pounders. The functions of the sloop or corvette were like those of the frigate – escorting, patrolling, attacking and protecting commerce.

The definition of the brigantine is as subject to overlapping and confusion as the sloop. It began life at the end of the seventeenth century as a square-sailed two-master mainly for carrying dispatches. It

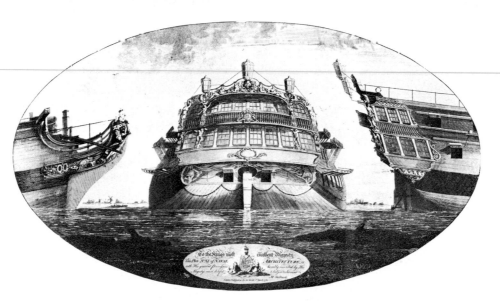

ABOVE *(left)*: *An English brigantine of 1750, by Clevely*

ABOVE *(right)*: *A man-of-war brigantine, by Brooking. Pictures of naval brigantines under sail are very rare – the jack and pennant indicate that it is one*

CENTRE: *Bow, stern and quarter of a battleship from Stalkartt's 'Naval Architecture' of 1781*

LEFT: *Two frigates before the wind, by Brooking*

OVERLEAF *(left)*: *The* Resolution, *1669, by Van de Velde II – a third rate of 70 guns*

OVERLEAF *(above right)*: *The captured* Santa Brigida, *with the* Naiad, *the* Alcmene *and the* Ethalion, *1800, by Whitcombe*

OVERLEAF *(below right)*: *'The Battle of La Hogue after Admiral Rook's attack', 1692, by Van Diest*

might have carried half a dozen or a dozen light pieces on its main deck. It could also be called a snow when the boom mainsail was hooped to a trysail mast abaft the mainmast. Inevitably, its size increased and its sail plan became more elaborate during the next century.

The cutter shared the patrol and dispatch duties also performed by the brigantine, but carried a single mast and a yard with a single square sail, over which was set a square topsail. In its developed and enlarged form in the later 1700s, an English cutter of 150 tons carried around twelve guns, a pair of carronades and one or two swivel guns.

The schooner was pure Dutch-American in its origin – a fast, two-masted vessel, fore-and-aft rigged, with the mainmast somewhat taller than the fore mast, but sometimes carrying square topsails on both masts. When the British seized New Amsterdam from the Dutch in 1664 (and changed its name to New York after King Charles II's brother), most of the Dutch settlers decided to stay on. Among them were many who had inherited the instinctive Dutch

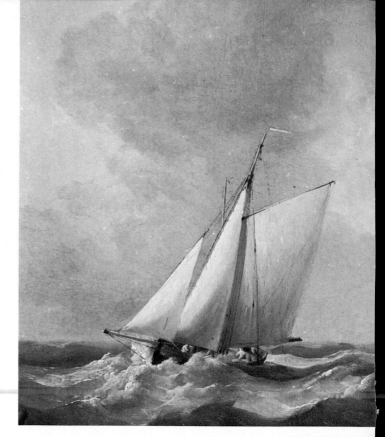

ability for ship design and ship-building. The building of fine sloops was a Dutch speciality, and from these was derived the first schooner. The story goes that the first genuine schooner with a triangular headsail was built at Gloucester, Massachusetts, in 1713. As she was leaving the stocks and entering the water, so it is said, someone exclaimed, 'Oh, how she scoons!' Overhearing this, her builder replied: 'Very well, then, a schooner let her be.'

By contrast with these fast and handsome small fighting ships, the bomb ketch was a crude and cumbersome but extremely efficient weapon carrier. It was pure French in its origins. Well-defended forts had always been a problem for cannon-armed men-of-war. When Admiral Abraham Du Quesne departed from Toulon on 12 July 1682 with a powerful squadron of galleons and galleys to deal with the pirate town of Algiers, he brought with him a number of *galiotes à bombes*, the invention of one Bernard Renau d'Eliçagaray.

Mortars firing primitive but large bombs had been used effectively in land warfare, especially for siege work, for many years. Their application to sea warfare was to have devastating consequences, in the narrow rôle to which they were necessarily restricted. 'The vessel built for this purpose,' wrote the nineteenth-century naval historian, John Charnock, 'was in burthen about 200 tons, constructed with every possible attention to strength, and was of much greater breadth in proportion to its length than was ever thought necessary. Its masts were two in number, the tallest being in the centre, the shorter in the stern, occupying the place of that which in ships is called the mizzen; on the fore part,

which was purposely left open, were placed the mortars; and, in order to take off or lessen that dangerous effect which it was imagined the sudden explosion of so great a quantity of powder fired in the necessary direction, and surmounted by a bomb, weighing nearly two hundredweight, would have on the vessel, the whole, or at least the greater part of the hold between the mortars and the keel, was closely packed and laid with old cables, cut into lengths for the purpose. The elasticity and yielding quality of the support obviated the apprehended inconvenience, and a trivial practice raised the art to a species of perfection almost unprecedented, so that a bomb vessel soon became one of the most dreadful engines of naval war.'

The bomb ketch was largely instrumental in giving the French complete control of the Mediterranean, and in keeping it until supremacy was challenged by the British Navy. But the bomb ketch was too slow and unhandy, its accuracy too speculative, for its shattering power to be used in ship-to-ship combat.

OPPOSITE: *A bomb ketch by de Passebon. This was really a square rigged three-master without the foremast – in its place was a short-muzzled cannon that hurled shells into enemy fortifications*

OVERLEAF *(above left)*: *Frigate action. Ship-to-ship actions were commonplace and often ended with the ships locked together, the guns pounding the ships to pieces from a distance of a few feet, while the crews engaged in hand-to-hand combat on deck and marksmen in the rigging did their best to pick off their opponents. Such actions often resulted in the total disablement of both vessels*

OVERLEAF *(below left)*: *A French and a British brig engaged in a ship-to-ship action. The tactic of aiming broadsides at the stern of an opposing vessel was a common one. Well-aimed shots would smash through the unprotected stern, sweeping along the decks and causing fearful carnage amongst the ship's company*

OVERLEAF *(right)*: *Detail of 'The Battle of 1 June 1794' by de Loutherbourg*

BELOW: *A late eighteenth-century Maltese cutter, showing clearly the single mast and yard and the sail arrangement, although the square topsail is obscured*

LEFT: *A late eighteenth-century French corvette, by Baugean*

OPPOSITE *(above)*: *A cutter close hauled, by Brooking*

OPPOSITE *(below)*: *An English snow-rigged sloop of 1720*

OVERLEAF: '*The Royal George off Deptford', by Clevely the Elder. Deptford, Chatham, Plymouth, Portsmouth and Woolwich were Britain's five arsenals at that time*

BELOW: *A snow, by Brooking, the boom mainsail hooped to a trysail mast abaft the mainmast*

ability for ship design and ship-building. The building of fine sloops was a Dutch speciality, and from these was derived the first schooner. The story goes that the first genuine schooner with a triangular headsail was built at Gloucester, Massachusetts, in 1713. As she was leaving the stocks and entering the water, so it is said, someone exclaimed, 'Oh, how she scoons!' Overhearing this, her builder replied: 'Very well, then, a schooner let her be.'

By contrast with these fast and handsome small fighting ships, the bomb ketch was a crude and cumbersome but extremely efficient weapon carrier. It was pure French in its origins. Well-defended forts had always been a problem for cannon-armed men-of-war. When Admiral Abraham Du Quesne departed from Toulon on 12 July 1682 with a powerful squadron of galleons and galleys to deal with the

pirate town of Algiers, he brought with him a number of *galiotes à bombes*, the invention of one Bernard Renau d'Eliçagaray.

Mortars firing primitive but large bombs had been used effectively in land warfare, especially for siege work, for many years. Their application to sea warfare was to have devastating consequences, in the narrow rôle to which they were necessarily restricted. 'The vessel built for this purpose,' wrote the nineteenth-century naval historian, John Charnock, 'was in burthen about 200 tons, constructed with every possible attention to strength, and was of much greater breadth in proportion to its length than was ever thought necessary. Its masts were two in number, the tallest being in the centre, the shorter in the stern, occupying the place of that which in ships is called the mizzen; on the fore part, which was purposely left open, were placed the mortars; and, in order to take off or lessen that dangerous effect which it was imagined the sudden explosion of so great a quantity of powder fired in the necessary direction, and surmounted by a bomb, weighing nearly two hundredweight, would have on the vessel, the whole, or at least the greater part of the hold between the mortars and the keel, was closely packed and laid with old cables, cut into lengths for the purpose. The elasticity and yielding quality of the support obviated the apprehended inconvenience, and a trivial practice raised the art to a species of perfection almost unprecedented, so that a bomb vessel soon became one of the most dreadful engines of naval war.'

The bomb ketch was largely instrumental in giving the French complete control of the Mediterranean, and in keeping it until supremacy was challenged by the British Navy. But the bomb ketch was too slow and unhandy, its accuracy too speculative, for its shattering power to be used in ship-to-ship combat.

OPPOSITE: *A bomb ketch by de Passebon. This was really a square rigged three-master without the foremast – in its place was a short-muzzled cannon that hurled shells into enemy fortifications*

OVERLEAF *(above left): Frigate action. Ship-to-ship actions were commonplace and often ended with the ships locked together, the guns pounding the ships to pieces from a distance of a few feet, while the crews engaged in hand-to-hand combat on deck and marksmen in the rigging did their best to pick off their opponents. Such actions often resulted in the total disablement of both vessels*

OVERLEAF *(below left): A French and a British brig engaged in a ship-to-ship action. The tactic of aiming broadsides at the stern of an opposing vessel was a common one. Well-aimed shots would smash through the unprotected stern, sweeping along the decks and causing fearful carnage amongst the ship's company*

OVERLEAF *(right): Detail of 'The Battle of 1 June 1794' by de Loutherbourg*

BELOW: *A late eighteenth century Maltese cutter, showing clearly the single mast and yard and the sail arrangement, although the square topsail is obscured*

The American War of Independence

The genesis of the naval power of America in the present century can be found in the maritime enthusiasm and skill of the early settlers as merchants, shipbuilders and mariners. Marcus, in his *Naval History of England*, has admirably set the scene:

The tough Yankee stock bred some of the very finest seamen and shrewdest merchants of their day. The trading and fishing fleets of these northern colonies were manned by successive generations of hardy, adventurous youngsters attracted to the sea by the lure of high wages. The keener spirits among them made voyage after voyage; acquired skill and experience; studied, qualified, and became masters and mates in their turn. Navigation schools arose in almost every port of consequence on the New England coast. Recourse and initiative were the leading characteristics of the able merchant interest who directed the manifold business activities of the northern colonies.

The boldness and the expertise of the American fighting sailor in the War of Independence, and later

in 1812, were derived from the generations of rugged experience of these northern seamen among the cod fishing banks off Newfoundland, farther north in search of whales to bring back to Nantucket Island, and from the long transatlantic voyages from New England to the ports of the Old World. At the start of the Revolution in 1775 the colonists could draw on a vast merchant marine of several thousand vessels, mainly of a very modest tonnage. Not one had been built with combat in mind. Orders were given to fit out a number of these with guns to serve as privateers and to harass British communications. In December 1775 the Continental Congress decided to build thirteen men-of-war. Although several fighting ships had been constructed in Massachusetts in the past, including a ship-of-the-line in 1690 and a frigate, the *America*, in the 1740s, for the Royal Navy, these frigates of 24 to 32 guns – the *Boston*, *Delaware, Montgomery, Trumbull, Congress, Providence*, *Effingham, Virginia, Warren, Randolph, Raleigh, Hancock* and *Washington* – formed the foundations of a

navy which 170 years later was to be the most powerful in the world. By 1778 all but four of these ships had been lost, but the new Continental Navy had added greatly to its strength through purchases, captures and new construction.

There was never any question of a fleet action between the Revolutionary Navy and the British. The British battle fleet, later to become the business of the colonists' French allies, was never in danger. But the depredations of the frigates and the smaller privateers among British merchantmen on both sides of the Atlantic became very serious, preying on commerce, intercepting communications, bringing terror and destruction to the merchant fleet, and supplying the patriot army with munitions, stores and clothing.

Attacks by American privateers – and there were many almost as evasive as the notorious John Paul Jones – on both sides of the Atlantic sent marine insurance rates rocketing, diverted naval effort to the provision of convoys, and gravely injured British morale at sea. Nor was the British Navy able to interfere seriously in the vital military and commercial trade between France and the American colonists before the French intervened in the war.

BELOW: *The* Serapis *and the* Bonhomme Richard. *John Paul Jones, a Scottish gardener's son, was the original hero of the U.S. Navy. With French help he fitted out two ships in which he proceeded to conduct operations against his old friends around Whitehaven, Cumberland, which he had known as a boy. He attacked an English convoy in the North Sea and after a fierce engagement captured the English frigate* Serapis. *However, she successfully defended the escape of the convoy*

OPPOSITE: *'The Battle of Lake Champlain', 1776. In this war on the North American lakes, Britain defended Canada against the newly independent America*

OVERLEAF: *'The* Serapis *and the* Bonhomme Richard*', 1779, by Paton. The inhabitants of Scarborough and Bridlington were able to witness at first hand from the cliffs of Flamborough Head Jones's fighting skill and tenacity in this action. The heavy shot of the* Serapis *quickly began to tell. The* Bonhomme Richard *received several hits between wind and water, and had most of her guns disabled or dismantled. In the circumstances Jones determined to close with the enemy. The hull of the American vessel was speedily reduced to splinters, but the British were unable to board because of the American marksmen in the rigging. The British captain was forced to surrender, but the shattered American privateer later sank*

American Frigates

No nation in the world has created a navy with greater success and greater reluctance than the Americans. Three times in their history – at the end of the 1700s, in the early 1900s and in the 1940s – the Americans have deemed it necessary, against their national inclination, to create a fighting fleet to protect their shores and their trade. On the second and third of these occasions they rapidly modernized and added to the strength of an existing fleet. In 1794 they had no nucleus on which to build, and the decision to do so was reached by a new, still loosely-knit nation whose mores and constitutional spirit were strongly opposed to military expenditure of any kind. It remains a wonder that this new fighting force, built with anxiety and parsimony by a people with a negligible fighting tradition at sea, turned out to be the most advanced and successful in the world, a tiny *corps d'élite* which had no peer during their life-time.

In 1793 the maritime condition of the Union was precarious. Following the conclusion of the War of Independence, American finances and trade were highly vulnerable. Even if America had wanted a navy, she could have scarcely afforded the construction of a single sloop. The surviving units of the old Revolutionary Navy had been sold off. Nothing remained. In 1793 France and Britain were at war again, taking liberties with American merchant shipping. The Barbary pirates were, as always, disrupting trade in the Mediterranean and demanding outrageous yearly tribute in default of which American ships were captured and their crews sold into slavery. In order to secure the release of these captives the government at one time had been obliged to build a warship, the *Crescent*, 'one of the finest specimens of elegant naval architecture which was ever borne on the Pascataqua's waters', load with her many valuable presents – including twenty-six barrels of silver dollars – for the Dey of Algiers, and hand over ship and cargo complete to this dictator.

'But out of the national humiliation,' wrote Spears, in his history of the United States Navy seventy-five years ago, 'sprang a new navy. The people who had called every legislator that spoke for the honour of the flag a blatant demagogue; the people who had feared naval tyrants, who had feared taxation, and who had argued that a small navy was worse than none – the peace-at-any-price men had been in a great majority.' But even the most ardent peace-man rebelled at the idea of building warships for foreign robber barons in order to obtain free passage for Yankee merchantmen. On 27 March 1794 the United States Congress reluctantly and by a narrow majority passed an act authorizing the acquisition or construction of six men-of-war for the protection of American trade. There were to be many hold ups before even this token force could be completed. And what use could it be, when six fighting ships were ready for their first commission? Privateers and pirates were still rife, and the vast fighting fleets of Britain, France and Spain were loose on the seas of the western world.

This is the real date of birth of the United States Navy. The man who was to be responsible for the overall conception of these ships believed that if they were properly designed for their task they could be of immense value. He was Joshua Humphreys, a Quaker of Philadelphia, who had been laying down keels for thirty years and was recognized as the ablest shipbuilder in the New World. President Washington approached Humphreys for his views, and these were delivered, in one of the most notable summaries of requirement in naval history, to the Secretary of War, General Knox.

OPPOSITE: *The* Independence, *by Schmidt*

OVERLEAF *(above left)*: *The* Constitution *blowing up the* Java, *1812, by Pocock*

OVERLEAF *(below left)*: *The* United States *and the* Macedonian, *1811, by Coates*

OVERLEAF *(above right)*: *The* Erie, *1824, by Camilierre*

OVERLEAF *(below right)*: *The* Constellation, *by de Simone*

BELOW: *The* Constitution, *engraved by Bowen*

'As our navy for a considerable time will be inferior in numbers,' wrote Humphreys, 'we are to consider what size ships will be most formidable and be an overmatch for those of an enemy; such frigates as in blowing weather would be an overmatch for double-deck ships and in light winds to evade coming to action. Frigates will be the first object, and none ought to be built less than 150 feet keel, to carry thirty 24-pounders on the gun-deck. Ships of this construction have everything in their favour; their great height gives them the advantage of sailing, which is an object of the first magnitude. They are superior to any European frigate, and if others be in company, our frigates can always lead ahead and never be obliged to go into action but on their own terms, except in a calm; in blowing weather, our ships are capable of engaging to advantage double-deck ships.'

These fighting ships had to carry a great weight of armament. Humphreys drew inspiration from the French masters. The French marine had cleverly cut down a number of their three-deckers – 'razoring-off' their two upper decks. These *razées* made immensely strong and steady, if mighty slow, frigates. Humphreys later wrote: 'As soon as Congress had agreed to build the frigates, it was contemplated to make them the most powerful, and at the same time the most useful ships. After the most extensive researches and mature deliberations their dimensions were fixed and I was directed to prepare the draughts; which was accordingly done and approved. Those plans appear to be similar with those adopted by France in their great experience in naval architecture; they

having cut down several of their 74s to make heavy frigates.... From the construction of [our] ships it is expected the commanders of them will have it in their power to engage or not any ship as they may think proper; and no ship under 64 now afloat but what must submit to them. These reasons are paramount to all objections, and annihilate opposition.'

These recommendations were accepted by the President and by the War Department – the Navy Department was not formed until 30 April 1798 – and the six frigates, the finest to be built anywhere at any time, were ordered to be laid down. They were the *Constitution*, built at Boston, rated as a '44', famed victor over the *Guerrière* and *Java*; *President*, blockade runner in the War of 1812; *United States*, another '44'; *Chesapeake*, which succumbed to the *Shannon* in 1813; *Constellation*, today a public memorial at Baltimore; and *Congress*, which captured thirteen British merchantmen in the opening months of the War of 1812.

ABOVE: *The* Guerrière *being captured by the* Constitution, *engraved by Birch*

OPPOSITE *(above)*: '*The capture of the President*', *1812, by Walters. From left to right the ships are the* Endymion, Majestic, Tenedos, President *and* Pomone. *She was overpowered after a long chase, and her name has been carried on in the British Navy.* HMS President *on the Victoria Embankment, London, commemorates the capture of a ship named after the President of the United States*

LEFT: *Perry's victory on Lake Erie, 1813, by Birch*

OVERLEAF *(left)*: '*The* Constitution *and the* Guerrière', *1812, by Birch. This action was the first between British and United States frigates and resulted in a victory for the American vessel. The broadsides of the British frigate were so ineffective that the* Constitution *won a new nickname 'Old Ironsides'*

OVERLEAF *(right)*: *The* Chesapeake *and the* Shannon, *1813, by Elmes. The* Chesapeake, *with a fresh untrained crew, was captured by the British frigate after a furious battle and was taken into the British Navy*

having cut down several of their 74s to make heavy frigates.... From the construction of [our] ships it is expected the commanders of them will have it in their power to engage or not any ship as they may think proper; and no ship under 64 now afloat but what must submit to them. These reasons are paramount to all objections, and annihilate opposition.'

These recommendations were accepted by the President and by the War Department – the Navy Department was not formed until 30 April 1798 – and the six frigates, the finest to be built anywhere at any time, were ordered to be laid down. They were the *Constitution*, built at Boston, rated as a '44', famed victor over the *Guerrière* and *Java*; *President*, blockade runner in the War of 1812; *United States*, another '44'; *Chesapeake*, which succumbed to the *Shannon* in 1813; *Constellation*, today a public memorial at Baltimore; and *Congress*, which captured thirteen British merchantmen in the opening months of the War of 1812.

ABOVE: *The* Guerrière *being captured by the* Constitution, *engraved by Birch*

OPPOSITE *(above)*: '*The capture of the President*', *1812, by Walters. From left to right the ships are the* Endymion, Majestic, Tenedos, President *and* Pomone. *She was overpowered after a long chase, and her name has been carried on in the British Navy.* HMS President *on the Victoria Embankment, London, commemorates the capture of a ship named after the President of the United States*

LEFT: *Perry's victory on Lake Erie, 1813, by Birch*

OVERLEAF *(left)*: '*The* Constitution *and the* Guerrière', *1812, by Birch. This action was the first between British and United States frigates and resulted in a victory for the American vessel. The broadsides of the British frigate were so ineffective that the* Constitution *won a new nickname 'Old Ironsides'*

OVERLEAF *(right)*: *The* Chesapeake *and the* Shannon, *1813, by Elmes. The* Chesapeake, *with a fresh untrained crew, was captured by the British frigate after a furious battle and was taken into the British Navy*

Trafalgar and the Last Days of Sail

This great and decisive fleet action was won by the superior spirit, self-confidence and fighting prowess of the British seamen, whose trust lay in their officers and in the righteousness of their cause. Except for ships captured from the French (like the *Tonnant* taken at the Nile), the British ships-of-the-line at Trafalgar were markedly inferior to the French and Spanish ships. There was no ship-of-the-line on the British side to match the mighty Spanish *Santisima Trinidad*, with its four tiers of ordnance, or the 80-gun *Bucentaure*; but a fatally high proportion of the French and Spanish officers were lacking in zeal, and many of the men who served under them were recently recruited and disaffected peasants without seagoing or fighting experience. They did not stand a chance against the seasoned and ruthless English fighting men.

The Battle of Trafalgar was not only one of the most decisive battles – by sea or by land – of the Napoleonic wars and one of the greatest naval battles

of all time. Strategically, it represented the culminating triumph of the British Admiralty in its mature experience and its comprehension of the meaning of sea power to an island nation. In the last battles of the 1700s, it had become clearly evident that long-established tactical principles were being dropped overboard; at Trafalgar Horatio Nelson relaxed formality to a degree which permitted extraordinarily wide individual freedom and enterprise among his commanders. The way everyone seemed to do just what they liked looked to be simple effrontery at the time, and astonished the enemy. But Nelson knew his foe and did not regard him very highly. Trafalgar, then, marked the full return of individual initiative to combat at sea; with the difference that now there was organization and communication behind the apparent confusion.

The position on the morning of 21 October 1805 was this: Admiral Villeneuve with his allied fleet of thirty-three ships-of-the-line (2,626 guns) had recog-

ABOVE: *'The Battle of Trafalgar', 1805, by Pocock, from the 'Life of Nelson'. As battle is joined Collingwood in the* Royal Sovereign *leads the English and is first to break the Franco-Spanish line (which can be seen travelling diagonally forwards from left to right). The back line of English is led by Nelson's* Victory

OPPOSITE: *The capture of Spanish treasure off Cape Santa Maria, 1804, by Pocock*

OVERLEAF: *'The Battle of Trafalgar', 1805, by Wilson*

nized that he could no longer hope to avoid battle, and drew up his ships as well as he was able into a single line (actually a crescent, and a confused one at that) headed north off the coast, with Cadiz some twenty miles distant in the north-north-east. A light wind was blowing from the west-north-west. The commander-in-chief, flying his flag in the *Bucentaure*, had ten ships ahead of him, and the rest of the fleet,

including Admiral Gravina's 'reserve squadron' astern. Decks were cleared for action. French and Spanish ships were arbitrarily mixed together as a precaution against the dangers of jealousy and recrimination.

During the night the allied fleet had been scrupulously observed by the British *Euryalus*, a new frigate commanded by Henry Blackwood, and at dawn the allied enemy fleets were sighted to the southward, distance nine miles.

Nelson at once formed his fleet of twenty-seven ships-of-the-line (2,148 guns) into two divisions, each in single column. His flagship *Victory* led in the northerly column, while Vice-Admiral Cuthbert Collingwood, flying his flag in the *Royal Sovereign*, led the lee column, with the assignment of destroying the rear of the enemy.

Collingwood's *Royal Sovereign* (100 guns), built at Plymouth in 1787, renowned for her dull sailing

qualities, had recently been refitted and copper-sheathed. In contradiction to her nickname, the 'West Country Waggon', she surged ahead. These silent anxious minutes of approach over a grey-green swell that was soon to be stained red and soiled with the sad squalid litter of battle, and the moment of confrontation and blasting first broadside, have been many times described by French and British writers.

After giving and receiving savage punishment, Collingwood was relieved by the slower consorts of his division, which penetrated the Franco-Spanish line and set about the *Fougueux, Monarca, Algésiras,* the *Swiftsure* and *Argonaute* and the others. 'See how that noble fellow, Collingwood, takes his ship into action!' exclaimed Nelson from afar, where he could just see the *Royal Sovereign*'s mastheads above the billowing smoke of battle. And Collingwood, at about this time, is reported to have called out to his flag-captain, 'What would not Nelson give to be here!'

Nearly an hour passed after Collingwood received his first broadside before the *Victory* closed with the enemy. This was the close action which Nelson had planned for so long, and which, within half an hour, was to result in his own death. This was the moment when not only the quality of the weapons and the skill and experience in handling them was to decide the fate of Britain and of Europe; here, at this time, amid the bloody turmoil and cacaphonous noise of battle (many gunners were never to hear again), it was nerve and fighting will that would prevail. A savage and fearsome gallantry marked the conduct of many of the Spanish and French officers and men. But the weight of disciplined skill and determination was too great, and further imbalanced by unworthy admirals. Far away to the north Admiral Dumanoir Le Pelley felt disinclined to become involved at all, and in spite of frantic signals from Villeneuve, remained out of gunshot range and slipped away safely with four ships-of-the-line. Admiral Gravina escaped with eleven more ships, a number of which saw scarcely any serious combat. The speed and accuracy of British broadsides, the British marines' skill at boarding the enemy and countering their attempts at boarding, and the faultless British seamanship, were all too much for those of the allies who chose to stay and fight to a finish. Nelson died with the certain knowledge that victory was his. By 3 o'clock the tide of battle was already turning, by 5 o'clock it was almost all over. Nelson had called for the capture or destruction of twenty of the enemy. By 4 November, when the errant Dumanoir and his four ships were at last caught up and captured, the total

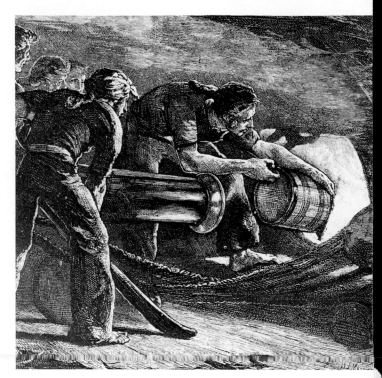

ABOVE: *The* Victory *at close quarters with the* Redoutable. *Between firing at the enemy the sailors threw water on to her to stop a blaze that might spread back to them. Fire was the most feared hazard at sea*

OPPOSITE: *Nelson fatally wounded on board the* Victory *at Trafalgar, by Dighton*

of French and Spanish losses was raised to twenty-two.

The victory at Trafalgar in October 1805 spelt the end of Spanish sea power for all time, and it took the French navy a quarter century to recover from the calamities of that autumn. But above all, the destruction of Villeneuve's fleet finally terminated any hopes Napoleon still nursed of invading England.

Trafalgar was the last decisive fleet action fought with sailing fighting ships, and these were not to be radically reshaped or radically improved in their fighting quality before the introduction of steam, shell and armour plate fifty years later. Although ships were shattered and dismasted by the fearful power of a full broadside of perhaps fifty cannon, 350 years after the introduction of gunpowder to sea fighting it was the destruction of men rather than ships (none was sunk during the battle) that decided the outcome.

Two men were especially influential in bringing the British fully-rigged, sailing man-of-war to its ultimate condition. They were Sir Robert Seppings, Surveyor of the Navy from 1813 to 1832, and his successor Captain William Symonds. Between them these two men were instrumental in applying science in the French manner to naval architecture, and bringing the standards of design of British fighting ships at last up to the level of the French. Both men were especially concerned with hull configuration and construction. Seppings introduced to the construction of a ship's hull a method of diagonal strutting, the need for which was brought about by the ever increasing size of the biggest ships. These diagonal timbers added greatly to the strength of the structure and diminished the hogging strains, which for so many centuries had created anxiety and exercised the ingenuity of shipbuilders. But these added timbers also greatly increased the weight of the ship and so reduced its speed – for which Seppings was harshly criticized. When Captain Symonds took over office his first need was to increase the speed of British warships. He went for a finer underwater section to achieve this, but necessarily had to increase the breadth on the waterline. Symonds' ships were highly regarded and satisfied the service's need for

greater speed, but they heeled acutely and made indifferent gunplatforms.

Not until the 1830s was there evidence of a serious renaissance in French design. When it came the French, as always, built well. But their superiority was no longer evident – and this time they were not above learning from others. The influence of Humphreys' American frigates was profound. The size, power, speed and excellent sailing qualities of ships like the *Constitution* had been noted among all shipbuilding nations. The British had built two formidable double-decked frigates, the *Leander* and *Newcastle*, in an attempt to match the American ships; and when France began building seriously again, like the British and Americans, she built big. *La Belle Poule*, for example, mounted her guns on two decks, and the size and number of her guns – thirty-two 30-pounders, two 80-pounders and twenty-six 30-pounder carronades – made her as formidable a foe as any 74 ship-of-the-line in Napoleon's day. She measured 209 feet overall.

ABOVE: *The* Prince, *1828, jury rigged at Portsmouth, etched by Cooke. She was the guardship at Portsmouth and seldom put to sea. It was said she was 'grounding on her beef bones'*

LEFT: *The* Caledonia, *1808, engraved by Dutton*

OPPOSITE: *The* Victory, *by Swaine*

OVERLEAF: *The* Nelson, *120 guns, 1809, a construction drawing by Pringle. As a result of lessons learned at Trafalgar, she was designed to be more powerful than her predecessors*

97

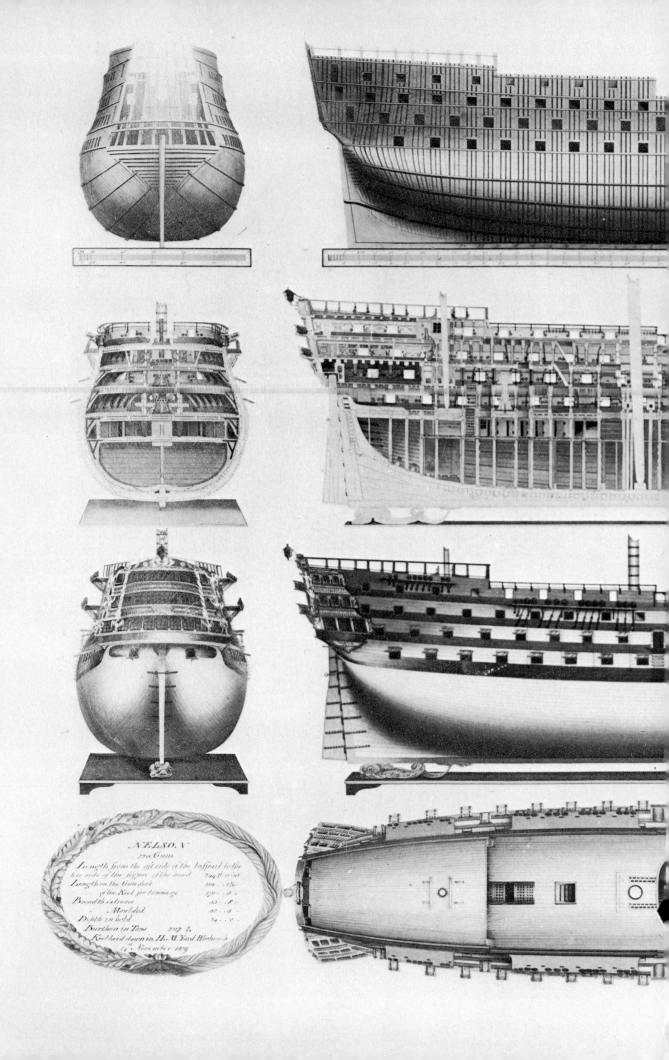

NELSON
170 Guns

Length from the aft side of the taffrail to the
fore side of the figure of the head   244 ft. 0 in.
Length on the Gun deck   205 ... 6½
of the Keel for tonnage   170 ... 0
Breadth extreme   53 ... 4
Moulded   52 ... 4
Depth in hold   24 ... 5
Burthen in Tons   2617 ⅔
Keel laid down in H. M. Yard Woolwich
14ᵗʰ November 1809

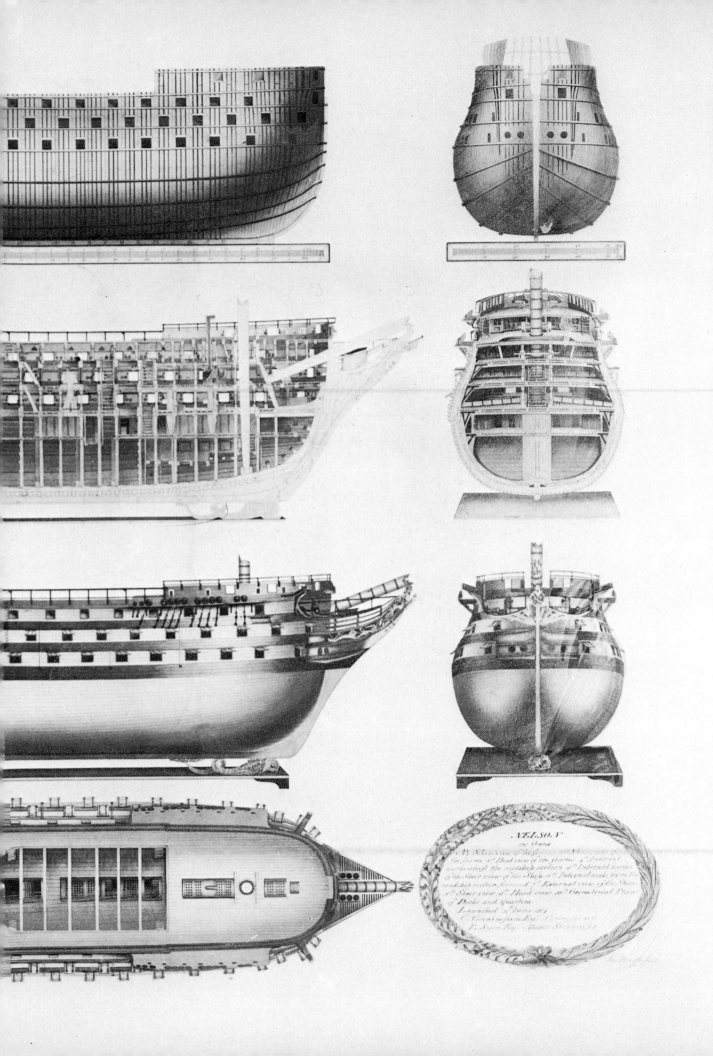

Chapter Three

THE ENGINE-DRIVEN FIGHTING SHIP

Transition and Compromise

The battleship of the 1830s really was mistress of the seas. She could meet any foe of inferior size, under any circumstances, with complete confidence. She could leave port and sail safely anywhere in the most unfavourable weather. She could remain at sea for as long, and travel as far, as any nuclear submarine of the 1970s. Much of the wonder and splendour of the great three-decker 'wooden walls' of the last days of sail lies in their arrogant consciousness of unchallengeable power.

It was a golden autumn all right, but a brief one. After its centuries of power, only a few decades were left to the wind-driven fighting ship. In less than half a century, the ultimate weapon at sea would be a graceless, noisy, low-lying slug of steel belching black smoke from a pair of dark funnels, nosing its way through the seas in fear that a single projectile or a new underwater form of high explosive might blow it sky high. The new weapons of science were to shape the heavy fighting ship during its last century.

The unlovely fighting ship of the mid-1800s came about as a result of momentous strides forward in three fields of science, all inter-related and concur-

rent. First, there was the revolution in ordnance; then in the fighting ship's motive power; and lastly in the material from which it was constructed. There was stout resistance to these sudden developments, and as a result, much delay in their whole-hearted acceptance. Conservative elements were supported by many early failures. Every time an iron vessel went down, a shell gun blew up or a thundering engine broke down it was a discouraging event, and those who had said 'I told you so' scored another point.

There was every justification for prejudice against the use of steam power and its transmission through paddle wheels. The engines were heavy, unreliable, inefficient and even dangerous. They did not only make a mess and a noise. They – and their nasty black fuel – took up cargo space in a merchantman and gun space in a warship. The fire risk was increased many times over. A paddle box made a large and vulnerable target. And one round of solid shot in the engine, or worse still the boiler – well, it was best not to contemplate such a catastrophe. But steam tugs were useful for towing big three-deckers

100

into or out of harbour, and in the 1820s and 1830s the French were especially progressive in applying paddle-transmitted steam power to larger warships – even to corvettes and frigates. These vessels made a new sight at sea, a sight that was fearsome or ridiculous, depending on the sailor's age and prejudices: a trim 1500-ton frigate like the French *Gomer*, fully rigged, sails taut in the wind, but amidships a single tall funnel belching black smoke and red hot sparks (a hazard if you like!) while attached, seemingly as an afterthought to both sides, was a huge semi-circular box, with the froth and foam from the rotating paddle wheel beneath it. This would not do, of course. The 450 horsepower of the *Gomer* was usable and even useful from time to time, but when it was not the paddle wheels upset the sailing qualities of the vessel. While the steam engine provided only secondary or auxiliary power, a form of transmission

OPPOSITE: *The* Rattler, *one of the first screw steamers*

BELOW *(left)*: *da Vinci's paddle boat designs*

BELOW *(right)*: *Robert Fulton's sketches for a steamboat*

less clumsy and inefficient than the paddle wheel would have to be found.

The history of the screw propeller, like that of the steam engine, is marked by numerous tentative and experimental projects, many of which got no farther than the drawing board. Among the claimants for bringing the screw form of transmission to a workable condition are the Swede John Ericsson, the English farmer Francis Pettit Smith, and the French engineer Frédéric Sauvage. It is Ericsson's name which has popularly endured, partly because he was a good businessman, and partly because he initiated other great advances in naval architecture. Ericsson, working in England, took out a patent for a submerged steamship screw in July 1836. Under the patronage of the American consul in Liverpool, Francis B. Ogden, he built a screw steamer (of this name) which was launched in April 1837. The British Admiralty expressed no interest in it, so Ericsson went to the USA, to his own enormous profit and that country's.

The development of screw propulsion went ahead fast in America. In Europe, too, some modest official encouragement was given to a form of transmission

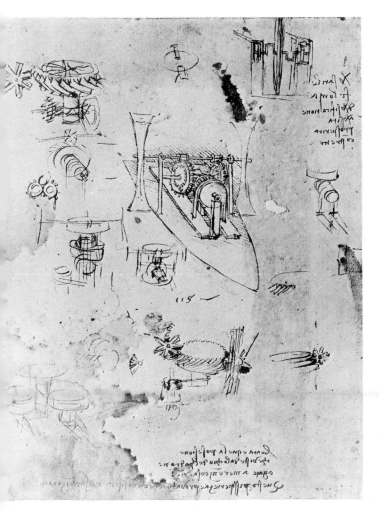

that patently possessed great advantages over the clumsy paddle wheel. Where Ericsson had failed to persuade the British Admiralty, Francis Smith had a modest success. The 880-ton sloop *Ardent* was converted while under construction to carry a 200 horsepower steam engine which was married to a Smith-designed two-bladed screw. It was launched in April 1843 as the *Rattler*. Two years later, she was lashed on a calm sea stern-to-stern with another steam sloop of equal size and power, but paddle-driven. With seeming effortless ease, the *Rattler* towed her fellow away at 2.8 knots. There could no longer be any serious question of the screw's superior efficiency.

By the late 1850s, the screw fighting ship, though still of course fully rigged, formed the backbone of the fleets of the major powers, and the paddle was left to the tug and smaller craft, which it nobly served for another hundred years. Reliance on the vagaries of the wind alone was now finished.

It was the mariner's deep and traditional fear of fire at sea which was one of the strongest obstacles to the acceptance of a furnace and boiling water and steam, in addition to large quantities of gunpowder, on board a man-of-war. The same perfectly reasonable anxiety delayed the introduction of the explosive shell. As far as the omnipotent British were concerned, there was the practical prejudice against the explosive shell because it might be effective enough to offset the sheer weight of numbers enjoyed by the Royal Navy. The French, for this same reason, zealously encouraged experimental work on shell guns and gained a temporary advantage.

Shells with short fuses, fired from 24-pounder cannon, had proved themselves at the Siege of Gibraltar. A British shipwright and artillerist, Sir Samuel Bentham, showed his employers, the Russian government, what could be accomplished by shell fire in the Sea of Azov in 1788. The Russian 'fleet', consisting mainly of longboats, but armed with shell-firing guns to Bentham's designs, annihilated a much larger Turkish force. The French began to take explosive shells seriously before the end of the 1700s, although the results were not seen in the naval war with Britain.

There were more experiments in America, where British bombardments of the New England coastal towns in the War of Independence, and later experiences in the War of 1812, pointed to the need for better shore defence. A certain amount of unsponsored shell gun experiment went on in England and among the minor naval powers during these early years of the century. But it was in France, a nation still smarting from the military and naval setbacks of the first fifteen years of the century, that the final catalyst occurred. Here was a country that had nothing to lose and everything to gain by disturbing the *status quo* in the fighting ship in its endeavours to regain its lost prestige and greatness. But not until the late 1830s was the shell gun generally introduced throughout the French Navy. Filled with a confused disquiet about the consequences on the one hand of following French practice and on the other of failing to do so, the British Admiralty hesitantly permitted the gun complements of some, but only a few, British ships to be converted to shell firing. The results of the Battle of Sinope, in which a Turkish force was annihilated by Russian shellfire, and the Crimean business a year later, settled the fate of round shot. By the 1850s the big naval shell gun had arrived, and this long cylinder of steel with its fearful promise of distant destruction was to dominate naval architecture and tactics for almost a century, culminating in the monster British and Japanese 18-inch weapons of the two World Wars.

Once the technical difficulties had been overcome, means had to be found to prevent or at least diminish the devastating results of a shell exploding within a wooden ship. The advent and acceptance of armour plate and the iron ship roughly coincided in time. There was strong resistance, both practical and emotional, to the use of iron for building ships. In spite of the success of Isambard Kingdom Brunel's iron transatlantic steamer *Great Britain* in 1838, and the successful bombardment by shellfire of the Kinburn forts in 1855 by a trio of French armoured steamships ($4\frac{1}{2}$ inches of iron over 17 inches of wood), Britain still placed her reliance on the wooden three-decker, even though they carried shell guns and auxiliary steam power, for the real fighting strength of her fighting fleet. No British iron warships took part in the Crimean War, and it was with misgivings and the utmost reluctance that the Admiralty ordered small armoured iron-built bombardment vessels after the successful French pattern. Experiments using solid shot conducted by the Admiralty in the late 1840s had proved that hits on the hull left iron plates with holes that were 'open and sometimes very jagged', whereas damaged oak planking could speedily be plugged, and was moreover partly self-sealing. The results of these experiments were still influencing British ship-of-the-line policy when the enormous (7,000-ton) three-decker *Victoria* was launched in 1859 – an uneasy compromise, a mass of contradictions and the last of her kind in the world. She was one of a class of four, all fully rigged yet with 4,300 horsepower engines, built of good solid oak yet carry-

ABOVE: *The Baltic fleet leaving Spithead, 1854. After a review before Queen Victoria, Admiral Napier led the fleet to the Russian War. Although he had proved a gallant officer in the past, Napier was unable to get his unwieldly giants to grips with the Russians, who were secure behind their fortifications and aided by rocks and fog*

LEFT: *The paddle frigate* Terrible, *1845, engraved by Papprill. There is a significant contrast between her funnels and black smoke, and the white canvas and beautiful lines of the three-decker. Steam frigates saw service in the Crimean War; the introduction of shell fire in this war was the death knell of wooden warships*

ing shell-firing guns. Except for the single funnel amidships they were little different in silhouette from Nelson's flagship at Trafalgar.

The French naval revival of the 1850s, like the earlier revivals in France and Britain, was the result of royal enthusiasm financing and encouraging the architects. After the uneasy alliance during the Crimean War, France and Britain quickly reverted to their customary condition of jealousy and hostility.

The ambitions of Napoleon III were boundless, and after the Orsini conspiracy crisis they included the invasion of Britain. Unlike Bonaparte, Napoleon III recognized the need to neutralize the British fleet as a *first* priority. And while he possessed armies five times more powerful than the British, he was at heart a navalist. He was also in the happy position of possessing a splendid ministry and the greatest naval designer in the world. In the Emperor Napoleon III and the designer Stanislas-Charles-Henri-Laurent Dupuy de Lôme, France enjoyed the greatest source of naval architectural inspiration in the world.

Dupuy de Lôme set about his greatest masterpiece, the fighting ship for which he will always be remembered, in 1857. At this time the balance of naval power between Britain and France was very fine. Both forces possessed great numbers of wooden three- and two-deckers, frigates, sloops and other smaller vessels, a number of which had been converted by the installation of auxiliary engines, besides a small number of frigates and others originally designed to steam as well as sail. (Unlike the British, the French had given up building wooden three-deckers.) The Emperor and Dupuy de Lôme – and all the young forward-looking elements in the French Navy – believed that the future ship-of-the-line, the final arbiter in naval combat, must be an armoured, iron, fast, steam-powered vessel armed with shell guns. Everything else was useless. If France could build enough of these quickly, it was claimed, she could gain command of the seas in any future war: l'Albion perfide would be annihilated. In March 1858 four of these first sea-going ironclads were ordered. Unfortunately (and this rather spoils the neatness of the pattern) France, unlike America, did not have the resources to smelt all the iron needed for these ships, and only one of them was iron-hulled.

This does not affect the historical importance of the project, nor did it diminish the acuteness of the anxiety it caused across the Channel. There followed the first of the Victorian naval crises in Britain. 'Such is the opinion of French naval officers,' wrote one British authority, 'respecting the tremendous power of these ships, that they fully anticipate the complete abolition within ten or a dozen years, of all line-of-battle ships.'

The first of Dupuy de Lôme's ironclads to be completed was the *Gloire*, an ugly stubby vessel of 5,675 tons armed originally with thirty-four 5-ton 16-centimetre guns and armoured with plates more than 4 inches thick backed by 26 inches of wood. She could steam at 13 knots, but was also fully-rigged, originally as a barquentine.

It was British naval shipbuilding policy at this time to avoid any radical innovation that might result in jeopardizing the quantitive superiority of the fleet and wasting the vast expenditure incurred in creating it. It was wiser and more convenient to await developments abroad and copy them and even improve on them. This could be a fairly leisurely business if the innovation was a minor one. The

laying down of the *Gloire* and her sisters was so alarming, however, that instant action was publicly demanded, and for once was swiftly taken. HMS *Warrior* was laid down in May 1859 as an armoured all-iron steam frigate, and because of her speedy construction was ready before France's *Couronne*, Dupuy de Lôme's own 'pure' ironclad. The *Warrior* was therefore, by a nice distinction, the world's first ironclad fighting ship. She was, moreover, superior in her speed and offensive power to her French rival, and with her sister ship *Black Prince* was successful in recovering for Britain the status and statistical superiority she had briefly surrendered.

By the 1860s the ironclad age had arrived, and the first stage in the revolution in all branches of naval architecture was complete. The ironclad, in all its hideous, fascinating wonder, was the new monarch of the seas.

In America, a minor episode in the Civil War registered in laughable inconclusiveness that a new age of naval fighting had arrived. The first ironclad battle in history occurred in Hampton Roads in March 1862; the fact that both combatants were freaks and incapable of serious ocean sailing does not deprive the *Monitor* and *Virginia* (ex-*Merrimack*) of their privileged place in history. The *Merrimack* was one of the formidable 1854 group of American wooden frigates, a 3,200-ton vessel armed originally with forty guns varying in calibre from 8 to 10 inches. During the war she was burnt out to the lower deck and sunk in Norfolk Navy Yard. Ingenuity and desperation raised her, her engines were somehow restored, and on to her was slapped an iron citadel with sloping sides. Her freeboard was so minimal that nothing else really showed, except a squat funnel and the ports for her 7-inch rifles and 9-inch and 6-inch smooth-bore guns. Her designers claimed her to be invulnerable, and so she proved herself.

There was nothing in the world like *Monitor*, the brainchild of that fiery genius John Ericsson. She consisted of an armour-plated hull 124 feet long, absolutely flat and with a freeboard of less than 3 feet. Her flush deck was broken amidships by an armoured rotating gun tower housing two 11-inch guns, a tiny steering house forward, two ventilators and two squat funnels. All except the gun tower were removed when cleared for action.

When at last these two bizarre vessels, prototypes of the ugly age of the ironclad they heralded, finally confronted one another, what could they do but harmlessly throw shot and shell, until the *Monitor's* ammunition was exhausted and the *Virginia's* gunnery officer, asked why he was no longer firing, could only reply, 'I can do as much damage by snapping my fingers every three minutes.'

This ironclad escapade marked the opening of one of the most prolonged and certainly the most expensive theoretical combats in the history of warfare, the battle between the ship-destroying gun and the ship-protecting plate of armour. It was to be a campaign of chemistry, metallurgy and ballistics fought out mainly in the laboratories of the scientists and only rarely and magnificently and tragically in real battle. The *Monitor* and *Virginia* affair aptly prefaced its folly and futility.

LEFT: *The* Alecto, *which lost a paddle versus screw contest against the* Rattler, *in 1845*

OPPOSITE (*below*): *The* Marlborough, *1854, by Pickering*

BELOW (*left*): *The Battle of Hampton Roads, lithograph by Currier and Ives, the first fight between ironclad warships, 1862*

BELOW (*right*): *The Russian coastal defence ship,* Novgorod, *1873; she had two 11-inch guns*

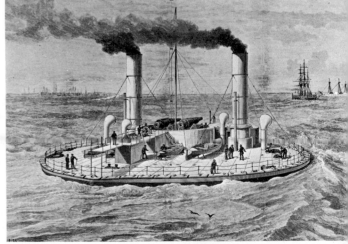

The Ironclad Triumphant

At first it seemed as if the mighty shell gun would prove itself a damp squib. At the Battle of Lissa in 1866, for example, the Austrian flagship *Ferdinand Max* rammed full amidships the Italian *Re d'Italia* at $11\frac{1}{2}$ knots, sinking her instantly. In this new age of technology, with its great engines and guns and armour plate, the ram had apparently proved itself as effective a ship-destroyer as it had been 2,000 years earlier. Overnight the ram became again highly fashionable. The construction of 'ironclad rams', the most weird form of fighting ship of all time, which had been actively used during the American Civil War, was everywhere stimulated. The ram bow was retained in the design of ironclads for many decades and for long after the effectiveness of long-range artillery had been proved in practice – even after it had sunk a Russian fleet at Tsushima in 1905.

Like women's fashions, no one could predict next year's shape and design for the ironclad. Some years it was all heavy guns, high speed and thin armour. The next batch might show special emphasis on protection, as if by spontaneous and simultaneous response every naval architect had got cold feet. After Lissa there were no fleet actions to test in action the theories of the designers. So they went on theorizing. The ironclad was increased in size, reduced, and increased again. The size of the gun followed the same pattern, emerged from its turret into an open armoured barbette, and with the revival of breech-loading, partly disappeared inside again; while the variations in its numbers and disposition were almost infinite. Sails were reduced in size and number, were dispensed with, had a brief revival, and finally disappeared altogether in the battleships

ABOVE: *A transverse section of the* Warrior

OPPOSITE *(above)*: *The* Warrior, *1861, lithograph by Dutton*

CENTRE: *The* Warrior, *which is still afloat in Pembroke Dock, Wales*

of the 1880s, to the undying distress and regret of those who had been brought up with them. The advent of the torpedo coincided approximately in time with the departure of sail, and was equally influential in shaping the appearance and development of the fighting ship.

The birth of the ironclad was a sudden affair, its evolution to its culminating point of maturity in the 1940s mainly leisurely and spasmodic. Two periods of acute naval rivalry, between France and Britain in the 1860s, and Germany and Britain in the early 1900s, provided the two great impulses forward with the *Gloire* and *Warrior*, and then the *Dreadnought* and *Nassau* of 1906 and 1909.

Development of the gun went on apace. Since the abortive *Monitor-Virginia* contest, the gunsmiths everywhere had been needled into finding a formula for a gun that could again sink ships. The dominance of armour plate was short-lived. With rifled heavy ordnance, the discovery of new means of building up the structure of guns, the advent of new and more powerful charges, and new forms of much more efficient shells, above all by the increase in its sheer size and weight, the gun began again to take command of the situation. In America the giant Dahlgrens were enormously destructive at short range. In Britain, the competition between the Royal Gun Factory at Woolwich and those two monarchs of ordnance, Whitworth and Armstrong, resulted in giant strides forward during the 1860s. Armstrong's breech-loaders appeared for a short time to be a real break-through, but they blew up too often and were very quickly discarded. The weight of the projectile rose from 50 to 100 pounds and more. Armstrong produced an experimental gun that threw a 600-pound projectile; and the calibre rose to 10 and 12 inches. Effective gun range began to increase, to 2,000 yards and then much farther. The day of the hundred-gun ship was finished, until its revival in the 1930s and 1940s with the need for multitudinous quick-firing small-calibre weapons to fight off aircraft.

The new big guns of the 1860s demanded a new approach to their siting and their protection. It certainly appeared to be wasteful to place these guns on each broadside, when their numbers could be halved without reducing the offensive power of the ship by siting them on the centre line in order to be able to fire on either broadside. The origins of the idea of placing a gun in a revolving cupola to fire on either broadside, like all the inventions of the 1800s, is obscure and controversial. But the two men chiefly responsible for its acceptance were Ericsson himself in America, and Captain Cowper Coles of the British Navy. Three years before the *Monitor* fought the *Virginia*, Coles had proposed a 9,200-ton cupola ship carrying twenty heavy guns in ten rotating turrets. All sorts of objections were put forward against this design, the most powerful and the most reasonable being that the masts and shrouds (for there was no question of doing without sails) must severely restrict the arc of fire of the guns. Coles persisted in his crusade and acquired the support of the press and many people of influence. One of these was Prince Albert, the Prince Consort, who lent his name to the first British sea-going iron turret ship which the Board of the Admiralty were finally persuaded to authorize in 1862 – a coast defence ship of a mere 3,800 tons armed with four 9-inch guns and with simple gaff sails that hardly interfered with the arc of fire of the guns.

The 7,000-ton *L'Océan* of 1868 mounted its main armament of four $10\frac{1}{2}$-inch guns in a central armoured redoubt in open armoured barbettes. By this disposition, it was no longer necessary to spread the thickest armour plate now demanded by the big new shell guns over the whole length of the ship;

instead *L'Océan* was effectively protected over her vitals – her biggest guns, her engines, her magazine and shellrooms – and with a reduced thickness of plate along the waterline: concentrate the armament, concentrate the armour. The British replied in 1869 to this French ship by laying down an ironclad, the *Devastation*, which marked almost as important a stage of development of the modern fighting ship as the *Gloire* and the later *Dreadnought*.

The cult of gigantism was seized upon by all nations aspiring to a first line battle fleet, and lasted for some twenty years. The battleship became a crude floating steel citadel, in which everything was sacrificed to functionalism and ferocity of demeanour. The Italians took things forward a further stage with the 10,000-ton *Duilio* and *Dandolo*. These two freaks contrived to combine a speed of 15 knots (the Italians have always liked fast ships) with four 15-inch 100-ton guns in two turrets arranged *en echelon* amidships between the two funnels and separated only by a single pole mast. Steel armour was used for the first time, and it varied in thickness from 17 to $21\frac{1}{2}$ inches, making the vitals of the ships absolutely invulnerable to the largest shells then in use. But because of its armour weight, which was some 25 per cent of total displacement, the rest of the ship had to rely for survival on watertight bulkheads and a thinly-protected deck. These were the first modern battleships to conform to the 'all-or-nothing' principle of protection, revived by the Americans in 1912 (see pages 134–6), and based on the belief that a well-built properly buoyant ship could survive to fight another day, however grievously damaged it might be, if its machinery and magazines are properly protected.

In this race of the giants the French entered *L'Amiral Duperré* protected by $17\frac{1}{2}$-inch armour, *L'Amiral Baudin* and the *Formidable*; Britain completed the *Inflexible* in 1881, carrying four 16-inch 80-ton guns, disposed in imitation of the Italians *en echelon* amidships, and protected by the thickest armour plate of all time – but as a last sop to the old brigade, with auxiliary sails again: she was brig-rigged. The maximum thickness of armour on the British *Inflexible* was 24 inches. This folly had reached the limit. Science stepped in to correct the imbalance it had initiated with the invulnerable *Monitor* twenty years earlier, and the giant gun it had brought into being. The metallurgists redoubled their efforts, and over the succeeding two decades Harvey in America, Krupp in Germany, Armstrong in Britain, Creusot in France, busied themselves with nickel and carbon and manganese in their steel, producing

ever more effective rolled plates which offered much greater resistance to penetration with much reduced thickness and weight in the armour.

The gunsmiths struggled against these new steels, and here too progress led to refinement and reduction in sheer size. The 12-inch muzzle-loaders in the British *Monarch* of 1869 could fire a 600-pound shell 7,000 yards twice a minute, while the French 27-cm. (10½-inch) breech-loader of the same date had a range for its 475-pound projectile only slightly less. The 16-inch muzzle-loaders of the *Inflexible* threw a 1,680-pound projectile which could pierce 23 inches of iron armour at 1,000 yards. Fifteen years later the same shell would have made little impression on American Harveyized steel half this thickness. In the 1880s the search was for higher muzzle velocity which gave better penetration at the same range. A slow-burning propellant was the answer, and because this demanded a much longer barrel, with all its attendant inconveniences when reloading, the British at last came back to the breech-loader, which had

ABOVE: *The* Minotaur, *completed in 1868, was single screw with exceptionally heavy armour and a speed of 14 knots*

been proved to be such an expensive *débâcle* some twenty years earlier.

All at once, in the 1890s, the scientists began to reshape the fighting ship again. They even changed the name: 'ironclad' went out of the vocabulary, and 'battleship' (a term which had never quite disappeared) took its place. The Americans laid down their *Indiana* class in 1891, with the elegant symmetry provided by two tall funnels, two masts and two 13-inch gun turrets, one fore and one aft. The British followed with the nine fine battleships of the *Majestic* class with a similar silhouette but funnels tight together side by side; the Germans with their strong and splendid *Kaisers*, the noblest if not the most powerful battleships of their day; the Italians at the end of the decade with a 13,000-tonner carrying the name of the great *Benedetto Brin*, himself the creator of the ugliest fighting ships of all time.

ABOVE: *The* Devastation, *1873, was the first sea-going 'mastless' turret ship. She had hydraulic loading gear. Here she is seen passing the old three-decker training ship, the* Duke of Wellington. *The* Devastation *represented the final justification of the work of Cowper Coles, who was drowned when his turret ship* Captain *capsized in a gale. The 9,300-ton* Devastation *cut free from the heavy, encumbering and now wholly superfluous masts and yards. Her central battery consisted of four enormous 35-ton guns in two turrets. She was protected by thick armour backed by teak*

OPPOSITE *(above)*: *The* Gloire, *1859, by Le Breton. She was the first French iron ship, but in fact her armour was hung over the wooden hull. The next ten years development in big ship design did not advance much beyond the standards set by the* Gloire *and the* Warrior, *and both programmes fell far short of expectation because of a shortage of either iron or money or both. A number of the battleships delivered to both navies were wooden hulled or were cut-down two-deckers partly iron-sheathed and armed with shell guns*

OPPOSITE *(centre)*: *The* Glatton, *1872, the first British single-turret ship. Her low freeboard made her a curiosity*

OPPOSITE *(below)*: *The* Conqueror, *1883, the new steel, armour-plated turret ship*

LEFT *(above)*: *The* Inflexible, *1881, had anti-rolling tanks, electric light, two 60-foot torpedo boats and new torpedo equipment, very thick armour, the heaviest guns in the service, and a minimal brig-rig to exercise the sailors. She was under the command of Captain 'Jacky' Fisher in the attack on the Alexandria forts in 1882*

LEFT *(centre)*: *The* Royal Sovereign, *1890, was the first class to exceed 12,000 tons*

LEFT *(below)*: *The* Majestic, *1895, was the most numerous class ever built*

The Torpedo

At the very height of the theoretical contest between guns and armour, the scientists stepped in with a new weapon which in the course of time was to alter entirely the nature of warfare at sea – all calculations, all strategical and tactical tenets, all accepted moral standards. The most destructive weapon of sea warfare in the great maritime struggles of the present century was the unmanned fighting ship, the crewless explosive ram – the self-propelled torpedo.

The locomotive torpedo began its life a little over a hundred years ago. At first it was not intended to be submerged but to operate on the surface, driven by steam or clockwork, and steered by ropes and guide lines after the manner of the Brennan torpedo. A Captain Luppis of the Austrian Navy was the inventor, but he did not make much progress before he called in a British engineer, Robert Whitehead. Whitehead worked at an engine plant in Fiume, where the machinery that powered the victorious flagship at Lissa was manufactured. When he saw Luppis's weapon he shook his head, said it would not work, and returned to his drawing board to devise a torpedo of his own. His prototype was tested in 1867. It was powered by compressed air, ran at 6 knots *under* the water at a (more or less) uniform depth for 300 yards, and carried an 18-pound charge in the nose. It was an erratic, unreliable weapon, but inevitably as its fearful potential was comprehended, rapid improvements followed. The British Navy bought the manufacturing rights for £15,000, and work on further improvement began at Woolwich. Speed rose to 20 knots and more, the range to 400 yards, and the destructive power of the charge multiplied many times over. Other countries began to buy manufacturing rights, and soon everybody was making torpedoes.

At first torpedoes were launched from ships' boats or launches, but by 1877 when the British Admiralty bought its first torpedo boat, the *Lightning*, a method had been devised of launching the torpedo from a tube on the deck. Eleven more boats of a type similar to the *Lightning* were ordered the following year. There was a tube right up in the bows and dropping gear abaft the tiny funnel. Speed was 20 knots, displacement a mere 32 tons.

Other naval powers followed the British lead, and among the most enthusiastic were the French, who began building a swarm of little torpedo boats with a speed of 23 knots, carrying a tube in the bows, a second on a turntable aft, and a pair of small guns. France possessed over 200 torpedo boats by 1892, and Russia, Germany and Italy each had over a hundred. All the smaller navies enthusiastically built or bought torpedo boats too, for in the torpedo they recognized the means of balancing up the numerical superiority of an enemy: for, above all, the torpedo offered, for the first time in the history of sea warfare, the intoxicating prospect of destroying an enemy fleet at negligible *matériel* and human cost.

BELOW *(left)*: *Robert Fulton's submarine* Nautilus, *1800. Fulton offered his services to both sides during the Napoleonic wars. For France he devised an explosive underwater missile which was tried against the British fleet without success. For Britain he demonstrated the effectiveness of his weapon by blowing up an old brig. The Royal Navy rejected his weapon, and Fulton returned to the United States*

OPPOSITE *(above)*: *The* Rorqual, *a conventional submarine*

OPPOSITE *(below)*: *The USS* Thomas Jefferson *SSBN 618 under way at sea*

BELOW *(right)*: *The Rev. Garrett's specification for a submarine, submitted to the Patent Office in 1878*

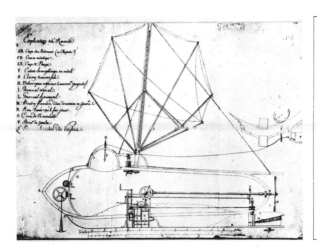

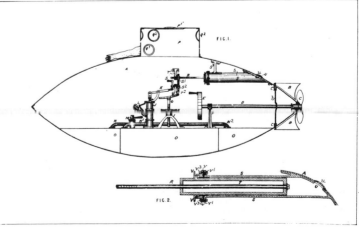

The effect of this on the minds of naval commanders, and their chiefs who increasingly controlled their actions from on shore, was profound and enduring. Such was the appalling and ever-growing weight of responsibility bearing down on fleet commanders that the anxiety they felt for the *preservation* of their valuable armoured fleet infected ships' commanders and all ranks. The boldness and aggression so splendidly evidenced in the Napoleonic wars, the War of 1812, the Dutch wars, and back in history to the galley actions of the Mediterranean, greatly diminished. The introduction of the torpedo was one of the chief causes of the cult of preservation rather than destruction in naval warfare from 1880 and right through the First World War.

Counter measures to the torpedo were energetically put in hand. These were of an offensive and defensive nature. The new big armoured ships were built with more substantial underwater protection, with double bottoms, armoured bulkheads and more elaborate compartmentation. Then, as it became clear that the fleet might now be attacked at sea and not only at anchor, much larger torpedo boats were designed which could sail with the fleet, attack the enemy with torpedoes, and defend the fleet from similar attack with their own guns. These were at first called torpedo catchers, then torpedo boat destroyers. The first were built in Britain in 1893, displaced around 280 tons, carried three torpedo tubes, and a 12-pounder and three 6-pounder guns. Speed was up to 28 knots, and it was calculated that they could catch any torpedo boat afloat within three hours of sighting.

High speed and the ability to inflict greater damage with a single blow than the largest gun were the unique qualities of the torpedo boat and 'destroyer'. Both increased rapidly during the last years of the century. In 1895 the French boat *Forban* was reported to have maintained 31 knots for an hour, and higher claims were made for a German destroyer. These speeds were accomplished by reciprocating engines. With the coming of the turbine, speeds rose still higher, and the vibration and noise aboard the little boats (which remained wet and cramped) became less intolerable. The turbine-powered *Viper* managed over 37 knots in 1899, and, even more impressive, held over 34 knots for three hours.

By the first years of the new century the rôles of the torpedo boat and the destroyer were clearly defined. They were both weapons of attrition, the smaller for inshore and harbour work (they were sometimes carried *on board* battleships), the bigger destroyer for sailing with the fleet at sea, defending

it and seeking by swift attack in numbers to divert attention and damage the enemy line by launching torpedoes at close range, escaping as quickly as they had come. The size and number of guns mounted by armoured ships for warding off attacks by these new torpedo carriers increased year by year. The *King Edward VII* class of British battleship, laid down in the first years of the new century, carried fourteen 12-pounders, the same number of 3-pounders, and a pair of Maxim guns to fight off the torpedo menace, besides ten 6-inch guns of the secondary armament, which would certainly be used against massed torpedo boat or destroyer attack.

The Whitehead torpedo was first used in large-scale combat during the Russo-Japanese war of 1904–5. Hostilities were opened – as at Pearl Harbor thirty-seven years later – by a surprise Japanese attack on the Russian fleet in Port Arthur. A handful of torpedo boats, in a few minutes of frenzied action in darkness, crippled two of Russia's best battleships and a cruiser, and entirely altered the balance of naval power in the Far East. Later in the war the loss by Japan of two of her six modern battleships in one afternoon by Russian mines suggested to some thinkers that the underwater weapon was to be the future arbiter of war at sea. But these lessons were soon forgotten in the crash of heavy artillery at the Battle of Tsushima – a classic gun duel in which the torpedo took no significant part. This provided a comforting, reassuring sound for those nursing doubts about the future of the big gun and its noble platform. General confidence in the battleship's massive weapons and her menacing profile was undimmed. She might no longer be the splendid sovereign of the seas she had been half a century earlier. Yet in 1905 her greatest days still lay ahead.

By the outbreak of the First World War, the torpedo boat had been replaced entirely by the destroyer for fleet use. Size, armament and speed had all greatly increased. Above all, the torpedoes themselves possessed a vastly increased power, speed and range. With its ability to destroy a 25,000-ton battleship at a range of 7,000 yards, it was little wonder

OPPOSITE: *Section plans and elevations. Early submarines kept near the surface at all times*

OVERLEAF: *The* Hermes, *aircraft carrier. The angled flight deck enables the carrier to fly off its aircraft at a greater rate. Britain has always led the way with its naval air arm, being first with torpedo bombers, aircraft carriers, jet propulsion for naval aircraft, and the angled deck (seen here) for quick launching*

ELEVATION

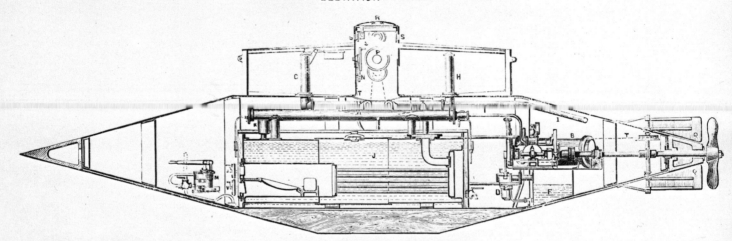

LONGITUDINAL SECTION

SCALE OF FEET

0 1 2 3 4 5   10

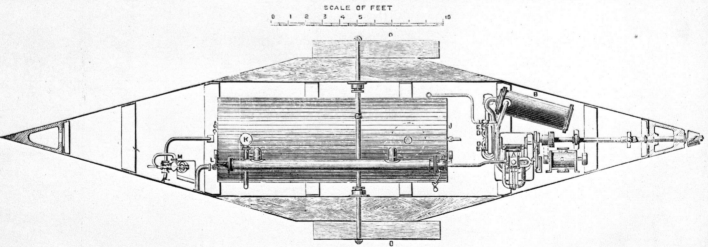

SECTIONAL PLAN

CROSS SECTION IN FRONT OF BOILER

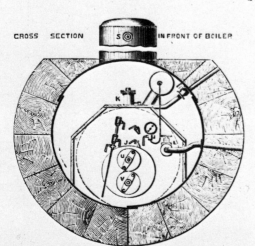

CROSS SECTION THROUGH ENGINE ROOM

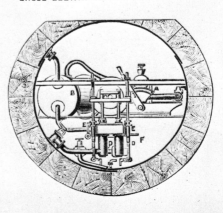

that the German and British commanders revised their fleet tactics in the event of a torpedo attack: the battle fleet was to turn away, to evade, and in the uncertain visibility of the North Sea, or in the artificially created smokescreen, probably to lose sight of the enemy – as happened at the Battle of Jutland.

The torpedo-carrying destroyer proved its worth during the First World War, but less in the function for which it had been designed than as a makeshift protector of the merchantman against the depredations of the most feared and most effective torpedo carrier of them all, the submarine. The great battle fleets of Germany and Britain, and later of America, could not venture to sea unaccompanied by their flotillas for defence against the destroyers and submarines of the enemy and for attack against his big ships. As the years went by, with only one major and inconclusive fleet engagement, and as the menace of the submarine against the commerce of the Allies grew more dangerous, the British Grand Fleet's destroyers were increasingly drawn from their inactive rôle of protecting a fleet that rarely went to sea, to convoying merchantmen and hunting their

hidden attackers. The Germans switched the crews, and the guns too, from their destroyers to their growing fleet of submarines.

The submarine began active life at the end of the last century when effective engines were adapted for use: electric when submerged, internal combustion petrol engines on the surface. In the years before the First World War the range, size and destructive power of the submarine grew with that of the destroyer and the torpedo itself. At first American and French craft were the most advanced. The British and Germans, who were expending such wealth and effort on their surface fleets, were reluctant to accept this new and potentially dangerous threat to their treasured battleships. The mind recoiled from such a sinister and barbarous weapon carrier, as it once had from the explosive shell, while ever-greater and more fearful shell-firing guns were warmly welcomed in the fleet. The eminent British admiral, Sir A. K. Wilson, described the submarine as 'underhand, unfair, and damned un-English', and his contemporary, Lord Charles Beresford, dismissed the submarine as a useless weapon because 'it is always in a fog'. Submariners were regarded with disdain as

members of an oil-stained force of outlaws – raffish and socially unacceptable. The demonstrations of the submarine's effectiveness at 'sinking' battleships on manoeuvres were treated unjustly. 'You be damned!' retorted one British admiral to a submarine commander who had three times 'torpedoed' his flagship.

It took the driving force of the radical and powerful Admiral Sir John Fisher to introduce the submarine, built under licence from the Holland company in America, into the British Navy. The German Navy, which in a few years was to come so near to annihilating with its submarines Britain's merchant fleet, was even slower off the mark. On the outbreak of war neither of these two great combatant naval nations possessed much faith in the power of the submarine except as a weapon for coastal defence and offence, and for scouting. It was left to the despised submariners themselves to prove the potential of their craft. Within two years it was the most feared weapon at sea. While the British Grand Fleet remained in Scapa Flow as the pivot of British sea power, controlling by its distant presence the surface of the northern seas, and exercising an almost complete blockade of Germany, German submarines in increasing numbers severely handicapped the Allies' war effort and brought Britain close to starvation and defeat.

Between the wars the pace of submarine development decelerated, although by 1939 it was a more potent weapon than ever, and defences against its hidden power had still not caught up. At one end of the scale were giants, bigger and more powerful than anything their most ardent champions could have envisaged in 1914. During the First World War the British had built a sort of battleship-submarine, armed with a 12-inch gun and an anti-aircraft gun. A few years later a cruiser-submarine armed with four 5.2-inch guns was launched. The French built the famous *Surcouf* with two 8-inch guns and capable of carrying an aircraft. At the other end of the scale, all the leading powers experimented with miniature submarines, manned by a crew of one or two. These consisted in some cases of little more than one torpedo with the pilot filling the place normally occupied by

OPPOSITE: *The* Hotspur, *1887, with her anti-torpedo nets*

BELOW: *The* Hornet, *1893, Admiral Fisher's first 'destroyer'*

Chas. PEARS.

FAR LEFT: *An Italian 'human torpedo' craft, 1941*

LEFT: *A British version, 1942, with the warhead removed*

BELOW: *'A British convoy on its way to Russia', 1942, by Pears*

the explosive charge, and a second or third real torpedo secured below. These were called 'chariots'. The Italians built brilliant and very effective submarines carrying limpet mines; the Japanese, characteristically, built suicide submarines, which were simply large torpedoes on which the pilot rode to his target and death. The Japanese were also very clever with their torpedoes, the 'Long Lance' oxygen-powered model proving its unique speed, accuracy and destructive power during the early period of the Pacific War.

German submarine development was similarly swift and efficient before and during the Second World War. The 'snorkel' allowed the much more efficient diesel engine to be used under water, and brought the submarine half way towards being a true submarine craft rather than a submersible – this conversion being completed with the introduction of nuclear power. Present-day American, British, French and Russian nuclear-powered submarines can remain submerged almost indefinitely and release their fearful new weapons without surfacing.

Infinite range has always been the target of naval architects. Today nuclear-powered submarines emulate the sailing warships which had no need to refuel.

RIGHT: *A Polaris submarine surfacing*

BELOW: *The USS* Picuda *submarine*

The Cruiser

The process of cruiser development in the late 1800s was logical and inevitable. The introduction of armour plate began it all. When the last of the steam-sail frigates received their inevitable plating protection against the new shell gun, they became armoured cruisers. Some were heavily armoured and, like the earlier fourth-rates of fifty or sixty guns, were fit to stand in the line. The smaller cruiser relied on speed for its protection. When this was matched by more powerful and equally fast armoured cruisers, light armour was applied to these smaller cruisers too. There then emerged the compromise small fighting ship, the protected cruiser, without armour plate on the sides, but with armoured decks and gun positions. These cruisers, too, possessed high speed as their first protection.

By the early years of this century, new cruiser construction among the great powers had settled into two types: small, light and very fast unarmoured cruisers, and armoured cruisers. The size, power and protection of the armoured cruiser rapidly increased. The German *Prinz Adalbert*, *Friedrich Karl*, *Roon* and *Yorck*, completed between 1903 and 1906, were of 9,000 tons and carried fourteen 8.2- and 6-inch guns. These fine ships were followed by the *Scharnhorst* and *Gneisenau* (11,600 tons, 8 × 8.2-inch, 6 × 6-inch, massively protected by 6-inch Krupp armour) which were to fulfil their rôle as commerce raiders so effectively and prove hard to destroy at the Battle of the Falkland Islands. The German armoured cruiser programme culminated in the greatest of them all, the 15,000-ton *Blücher*, armed with twelve 8.2-inch and eight 6-inch guns, which could steam at 25 knots, and five years after her completion survived an appalling hammering by British 12-inch and 13.5-inch shells at the Dogger Bank before she was sent to the bottom by torpedoes.

The ultimate American armoured cruisers (the *Washington* class) were scarcely smaller than the *Blücher*, boasted four 10-inch guns as their heaviest armament, and were inferior to the German ship only in speed. But the most remarkable of all armoured cruisers originated in Italy, and in the brilliant mind of the greatest naval architect of his day, Colonel Vittorio Cuniberti. His *Vittorio Emanuele* class of four ships, laid down between 1901 and 1903, and described by Fred T. Jane in his annual *Fighting Ships* as 'the ideal armoured cruisers', were almost small, fast battleships, with a displacement of 12,000

BELOW: *The* Ajax, *1934, in the River Plate. Five years later the* Ajax *took part in the engagement which resulted in the destruction of the pocket battleship* Graf Spee

tons, a speed of 21 knots (slower than most armoured cruisers but much faster than any battleship), an armament of twelve 8-inch and two 12-inch guns, and a main armoured belt on the waterline no less than 10 inches thick. Part of their secret of high speed, heavy armament and armour lay in Cuniberti's method of girder-like construction and the use of asbestos in place of wood in the interior fittings as another means of saving weight.

The life of the armoured cruiser in this century was a brief and mainly tragic one. She always was a hybrid, and with the *Dreadnought* revolution in 1906, the coming of the Dreadnought-type all-big-gun cruiser – the battle cruiser – instantly made every armoured cruiser obsolete: dangerously obsolete, for this class of vessel suffered grievously when struck by heavy shell, as at Dogger Bank and Jutland.

The functions of the armoured cruiser were twofold. Firstly, to act individually as commerce-raiders and commerce-raider destroyers, secondly to operate together with the fleet as a scouting wing. In this second capacity they were intended to be fast enough to escape from the big guns of the battleships and also to deal with light cruisers. The ideal light cruiser, however, could escape from the armoured cruiser, and with its superior speed scout ahead and also help

to destroy the destroyer flotillas. The light cruiser of the period before the First World War possessed a modest armament of guns of from 3-inch to 6-inch calibre, was protected only by an armoured deck, and could make from 24 to 26 knots. These were perhaps the most elegant and satisfactory fighting ships built at this time.

The armoured cruiser reappeared in revised and re-named form after the First World War as the Heavy Cruiser. The Washington Treaty of 1922 limited the cruiser to 10,000 tons; above this displacement they became classified as capital ships, which were restricted among the signatories by number, and by displacement to 35,000 tons. It therefore appeared sensible to build every cruiser to this limit, armed with 8-inch guns (the maximum Treaty calibre), armour them modestly, and give them sufficient speed to escape from the contemporary battleships. The result was a generation of mainly uniform heavy cruisers which by the time war came again were quite as anomalous as their predecessors because the battleship had now caught them up in speed, and the de-

LEFT: *HMS* Lion, *the last conventional British cruiser*

BELOW *(left)*: *The destroyer* Devonshire

BELOW *(right)*: *The* Devonshire *firing a guided missile*

Projekt (1897)

Kreuzer III Classe.

Länge	95	m
Breite	11,5	„
Tiefgang	5	„
Deplacement	2650	Tons
Maschinen	7000 HP	= 19,5 Knoten
Kohlen	400	Tons

8 — 12 cm L/35 S.K.
8 — 5 cm „ „ „ „
1 ↓ Bug
1 ↑ Heck
2 ↗ Brs.

Deck 25/50 m m
Comdth: 100 m m

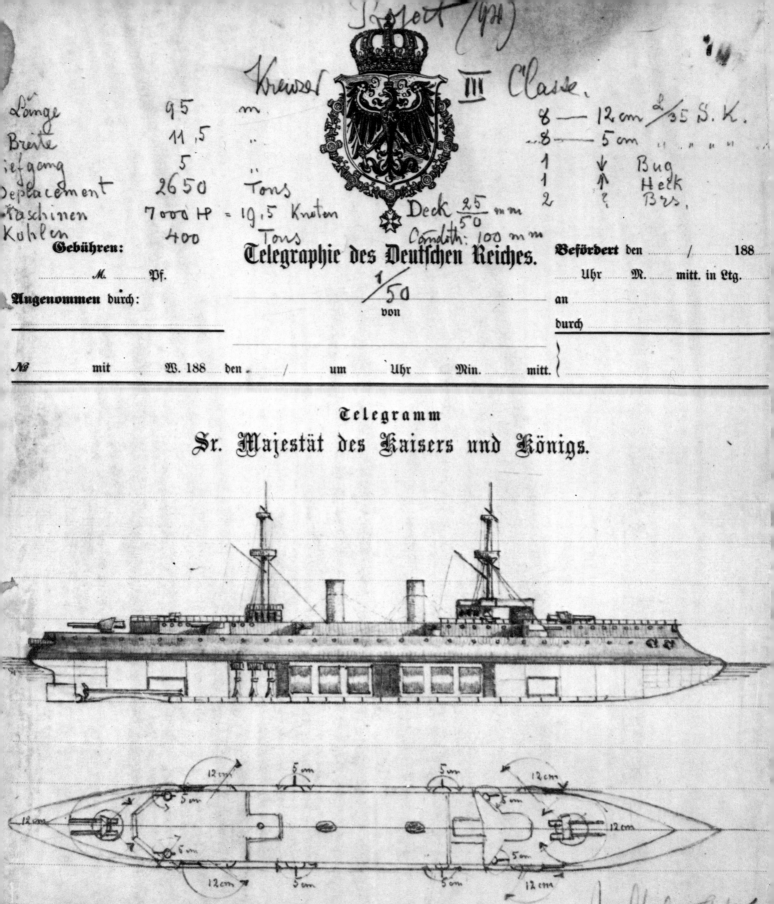

Telegraphie des Deutschen Reiches.

1/50
von

Gebühren:
M. Pf.

Angenommen durch:

Befördert den / 188
Uhr M. mitt. in Ltg.

an

durch

№ mit W. 188 den / um Uhr Min. mitt.

Telegramm
Sr. Majestät des Kaisers und Königs.

12 cm   5 cm   5 cm   12 cm
5 cm   5 cm
12 cm   12 cm
5 cm   5 cm
12 cm   5 cm   5 cm   12 cm

Fjärland.   12/VIII 94

126

velopment of airpower had made them even more vulnerable. Nonetheless, by ingenuity, cheating, and designing for local commitments only, some remarkable heavy cruisers were built between the wars. The British and Americans built conservatively. Their defence requirements called for vessels capable of meeting all weather conditions from the North Sea and the Mediterranean, the Indian Ocean and the Pacific, to the Atlantic in winter. Provision had to be made for a large fuel capacity, for outstanding seaworthiness, and for comfortable habitation for long periods. Representative of this new breed of heavy cruiser in America were the *Pensacola* of 1929 and the *Augusta* of 1931. They were armed with nine or ten 8-inch guns in centre-line turrets, a still-modest quota of anti-aircraft guns, with a thin skin of armour on the decks and along the waterline, with a speed of 32 knots, a radius of action of 13,000 miles, and several seaplanes for reconnaissance. Their intended rôle was to run down enemy cruisers and destroyers and act as 'eyes of the fleet' as their predecessors had done in the First World War. Their British contemporaries were the 'County' class, completed between 1927 and 1930. These much-criticized flush-decked vessels, with their three funnels and high freeboard, possessed a stately grace about them that was in

ABOVE: *The guided missile cruiser USS* Canberra *launching a surface-to-air Terrier missile*

LEFT: *A sketch for a cruiser III class by Kaiser Wilhelm in 1894, on an old Imperial telegraph form*

keeping with the Imperial responsibilities they were designed to uphold. They were the last of the British 'flag-showers', comfortably habitable in all climates, and with an operating range of over 10,000 miles. Like the armoured cruisers they succeeded, they proved highly vulnerable in combat circumstances not envisaged at the time Sir Eustace Hugh Tennyson d'Eyncourt drew up their design.

Italian strategic requirements were entirely different from those of any other major naval nation. As in the days of Roman and Venetian power, speed and flexibility of operation in the more kindly climatic conditions of the Mediterranean were the first needs. No other fighting ships of other nations, including their fastest destroyers, could match the Italian *incrociatori* of the 1920s and 1930s. The *Trieste* and *Trento* set the pattern. Like the British 'County' class, they carried eight 8-inch guns in paired turrets on the centre line. Their low profile with two squat funnels hinted at once at their remarkable maximum speed of some 38 knots, and they were also better protected with armour than the British ships. But like the galleys of old, they were essentially Mediterranean ships. They could not have withstood the rigours of winter North Atlantic convoy work that the British ships endured in the 1940s, nor could they have remained at sea for so long.

The Japanese and the Germans, while signatories to limiting treaties, and claiming to meet the restrictions they imposed, were quick to discover means of evading them. Some of their 8-inch-gunned heavy cruisers exceeded the treaty displacement of 10,000

tons by almost 50 per cent. The architects' problems of compromise were therefore greatly eased, and both these naval powers produced heavy cruisers as large and formidable as the *Blücher* of 1909, and far better equipped to match up to the new weapons of destruction devised after their completion. The Japanese *Nati* class completed in the late 1920s carried ten 8-inch and numerous light anti-aircraft guns, four seaplanes on catapults, could achieve over 33 knots and were substantially armoured. Like all their Japanese contemporaries, their low profile, complex superstructure, and heavily raked and often trunked funnels combined to give an appearance of fearsome and intimidating aggressiveness.

The French never regained in the 1900s their earlier gift for superior ingenuity and technical excellence in naval architecture. Their cruisers between the wars were, however, characterized by good sense, taste and grace. At first the French Ministry of Marine succumbed to the temptation of building up to the 10,000-ton 8-inch-gun limits of the Washington Treaty. The *Duquesne* had a main armament of eight heavy guns, very light protection and a speed intended to match – though it failed – that of the contemporary Italian cruisers. But at the same time France built lighter cruisers carrying 6.1-inch main armament, and vessels like the *Duguay-Trouin*, completed in 1926, set the pattern of cruiser development in the 1930s.

As war in the Atlantic, Pacific and Mediterranean became more imminent in the 1930s, all the great powers likely to be involved authorized massive programmes of cruiser construction. The shadow of the bomber and torpedo plane fell heavily over the designers' drawing boards at this time, and cruiser characteristics tended more than ever to high speed, a complement of reconnaissance or bombing cata-

pulted aircraft, an ever-larger number of light anti-aircraft guns and a main armament of 5-inch to 6-inch guns with a high rate of fire capable of being used against air or surface targets. Such a vessel was the United States light cruiser, *Brooklyn*, completed in 1938, which combined substantial protection against bombs and torpedoes with a speed of 33 knots, fifteen 6-inch guns in five triple centre-line turrets, and numerous batteries of medium and light anti-aircraft guns. Six aircraft were stowed neatly in a hangar and ready for catapulting from her stern. The French were busily building similar vessels at the time of the German invasion in 1940, when the British had already completed numerous 6-inch-gunned light cruisers which were to do invaluable service in numerous capacities during the next five years of war. The most spectacular cruisers of all time were built by the Italians in the late 1930s. Of very light construction, with negligible protection yet formidable dual-purpose gunfire ranging from 5.3-inch to 20 mm., they were capable of over 40 knots.

Like all its contemporary classes of fighting ship, the iron- and steel-hulled cruiser has suffered from the rapid pace of scientific development. In the First World War the superior guns and speed of the battle cruiser (see page 137) made the armoured cruiser a floating coffin in action. In the Second World War the cruiser was forced to sustain the onslaughts of the submarine and the aircraft, especially in the Mediterranean and the Pacific. The cruiser fought back with new radar devices, armoured decks, and more and more anti-aircraft guns. Her class suffered grievously, especially in the Japanese and the British navies.

Some were modified into pure anti-aircraft cruisers and a handful were built exclusively for this rôle. She survives to this day in a number of navies with a mixed armament of guns, rockets and guided missiles, and in her ultimate form as the 14,200-ton nuclear powered guided missile cruiser *Long Beach* with its fearful ram-jet propelled missiles which can carry atomic warheads and engage subsonic or supersonic targets.

LEFT: *Detail of 'Bombardment of a coast by HM ships* King George V *and* Duke of York*', by Eurich*

BELOW: *The USS* Springfield, *CLG 7, 1944*

The Dreadnought

From the holocaust of the Battle of Tsushima in 1905 European and American naval thinkers drew the conclusions that were to shape the nature of the fighting ship for the rest of its life. Tsushima proved the futility of mixing gun calibres, and that only the biggest gun was a ship-destroyer. Those thinkers who had been advocating for some time privately and occasionally publicly for an all-big-gun battleship saw their beliefs magnificently confirmed.

Like every great step forward in the development over the centuries of the fighting ship, there was nothing wholly 'new' about the single armament or all-big-gun Dreadnought type battleship. People had been thinking about them for years, and as we have noted all-big-gun ships of a grotesque nature were built some thirty years earlier. After years of experiment with every possible heavy gun permutation, a body of opinion in every navy was beginning to recognize that the mixed-armament battleship was nearing the end of its development. In the opening years of the new century battleships with a uniform armament of the largest guns were advocated by the American Bureau of Construction, in Italy by the advanced thinker Colonel Cuniberti, in Britain by Admiral Sir John Fisher. The Germans and even the Russians were known to be thinking along similar lines. Britain, with her overwhelmingly powerful Navy and vast maritime responsibilities, began to recognize the dangers.

It was left to Fisher to take action. This was no time, Fisher concluded, to conform to the traditional British policy of allowing others to move first and answering herself with more numerous ships. Fisher believed that the pace of competition with Germany made it national suicide to allow anyone to steal a march on his beloved Royal Navy. On the ninety-ninth anniversary of the Battle of Trafalgar, 21 October 1904, Fisher took up his duties as First Sea Lord. He immediately set up a Committee on Designs, which drew up plans for the rapid construction of a battleship that would make all others afloat or building obsolete. Less than a year after Fisher took office, this battleship was laid down at Portsmouth.

Fisher had prepared his plans with infinite care as well as unprecedented speed. Many of the vital materials of construction were made ready beforehand, the ship's guns (the construction of which was such a long and elaborate process that it often governed the building period of a heavy ship) were ruthlessly plundered from a pair of mixed-armament battleships already under construction. Nothing was allowed to delay the building of the new vessel. She was launched in a little over four months and was on her trials a year and a day after her keel had been laid. From stem to stern she was an inspired fighting ship. Not only did she boast ten heavy guns when no other battleship carried more than four of the largest calibre; she was also the biggest battleship in the world, the fastest, and the first large warship anywhere to be turbine-powered – Fisher's final master-stroke. At the same time she was adequately armoured with a belt eleven inches thick at the waterline, and was specially protected against torpedo attack. When she steamed off on her trials – she did 21.6 knots – she was the cynosure of every navy in the world.

It is true that HMS *Dreadnought* of 1906 created a revolution in naval architecture. And the drama of the revolution was greatly increased by the magnificently conducted staff work surrounding her construction and the triumphantly strident tone in which her imposing size, speed and gunpower were announced to the world. There were many critics of the *Dreadnought*, which made obsolete not only the existing battleships of Britain's potential enemies but her own as well. And because Britain had so many more than anyone else, the *Dreadnought* represented greater wasted tonnage to the country which had built her than to any of her rivals. The *Dreadnought* controversy raged for years in Britain. But the final, incontrovertible argument in support of Fisher's decision was that *other nations were already building all-big-gun ships too*, although this was not known publicly in Britain at the time. Both the Japanese and the Americans had laid down all-12-inch-gunned battleships early in 1905. Due to supply difficulties, the Japanese ships were not completed for five years, and then had to make-do with mixed 10-inch and 12-inch guns, and the Americans took more than four years to build the *South Carolina* and *Michigan*. But the revolution had already begun, even before the *Dreadnought* herself took to the water, and with her the generic name for a class of battleship which was to endure for as long as her kind.

A Dreadnought 'race' was inevitable. The pace was set by Britain. One of Admiral Fisher's many pungent catch phrases, which he repeated in his staccato manner on every possible occasion, was: 'Build few and build fast, each one better than the last.' Britain's shipbuilding resources were unmatched anywhere in the world, and Fisher saw to it that Britain did build fast so that her lead in the drive to Armageddon could be maintained. Some

thirty more British Dreadnoughts were completed before the outbreak of war eight years after the *Dreadnought* herself was commissioned. On every lap of the race with Germany, Britain remained ahead numerically and, ship by ship, statistically as well.

It was ships like the five *Queen Elizabeth* class of 15-inch gunned battleships that appeared to justify the maritime arrogance of Britain in the face of the giant Dreadnought competition going on all over the world. Fine-looking ships in great numbers and armed with the greatest guns, and with names like *Valiant, Thunderer, Hercules* and *Audacious*, could not fail to seem splendid and fearsome and provocative. It was partly for this reason, and also because she was quite lacking in any naval history and tradition, that the spirit of the German Navy in 1914 was tempered by a sense of inferiority. There was little *matériel* reason for this, except on paper. Between 1909 and 1916 von Tirpitz created a magnificent force of fighting ships mainly superior in quality and only slightly inferior in numbers to the British Navy.

The rapid construction of the *Dreadnought* upset the German plans as completely as Fisher had intended. Not only had the keels been laid for more mixed-armament battleships, but new ships to compete with the *Dreadnought* would require the widening of the Kiel Canal between the Baltic and the North Sea – a formidably expensive and long undertaking.

The German architects responded with an all-big-gun design that appeared to be inferior to the British contemporaries. While the *Nassau*, completed in 1909, carried twelve 11-inch guns against the *Dreadnought*'s ten 12-inch, only two of the turrets were on the centre line against the *Dreadnought*'s three, and the weight of main armament broadside of the British ship was therefore greater. She was also slower and smaller than her British rival. But the *Nassau* and all her successors scored heavily in their ability to resist both shell and torpedo. The ability to withstand intensive and sustained shellfire came to be recognized in the British Navy as a formidable characteristic of every German Dreadnought. From the *Lützow* at Jutland in 1916 to the *Scharnhorst* in 1943, the story was the same. German heavy ships could be reduced to a shambles by

shellfire without succumbing, and it required a number of torpedo hits as well to send them to the bottom. By contrast, British battleships proved themselves fatally vulnerable to mines, a few shell hits sufficed to destroy British battle cruisers in both world wars because they were inadequately protected horizontally against 'plunging fire' (projectiles fired from a great range falling almost vertically).

German Dreadnought development during von Tirpitz's period of office culminated in the battleships *Baden* and *Bayern*, which with their uncompleted sister ships were laid down in answer to the British *Queen Elizabeth*s. Displacement was up to 28,000 tons, speed to over 22 knots, and there were eight 15-inch guns, all on the centre line, four of them in superimposed turrets. Armour plate was almost 13 inches thick on turrets and side belt.

France, Italy, Austria – Hungary, Russia and minor powers like Spain, Turkey, Greece and even the South American republics all ordered Dreadnoughts during the height of the fever from 1907 to

ABOVE: *The* Dreadnought, *1906, an all-big-gun high-speed battleship; she was built in a year and a day, and gave her name to a new breed of fighting ship*

OPPOSITE: *The German battle cruiser* Derfflinger, *1911. She took a terrible hammering at Jutland yet managed to limp home half full of water and with most of her guns out of action*

1914. Shipbuilders and ordnance works the world over profited, and the output of steel in the industrial nations multiplied many times. But long before the fleets of Germany and Britain clashed in the North Sea, a new and fearsome rivalry for dominance of the Pacific had gathered speed. The Japanese were bursting with self-confidence and eagerness to develop the new technological skills they had recently acquired. And as a result the Americans were becoming increasingly worried about their interests in Asia. The Japanese Navy which had won at Tsushima had been largely built in British yards. Japanese apprentice technicians had watched the riveting of every plate, the construction of every

gun. They learned well, and hastened home. While the war with Russia was still raging, the first heavy armoured ships were laid down in Japanese yards – a pair of powerful armoured cruisers with 12-inch and 6-inch guns. Her first two 'pure' Dreadnoughts were laid down in 1909. Six more followed between 1911 and 1913. Nor were these fighting ships pale imitations of foreign practice. They were of ingenious design, were fast and exceptional in their gun-power and protection. The *Fuso* and *Yamashiro* of the 1911–12 Emergency Expansion Programme displaced over 30,000 tons, were 700 feet long, carried an all-centre-line armament of twelve 14-inch guns – supported by sixteen 6-inch – and steamed at 24.7 knots on their trials. By 1920 Japan had completed battleships carrying 16-inch guns – the first in the world – and giant battleships and battle cruisers with 16-inch and even 18-inch guns were being contemplated before the Washington Conference called a halt.

Neither in 1916 nor in 1940 could Japan hope to equal the fighting ship building potential of the United States. Japanese strategy in the Pacific was similar in many respects to that of Germany in the North Sea. Both powers hoped to whittle down the superior strength of the enemy by striking at units or detachments with greater forces and by underwater (mines and submarines) and later air (bombs and torpedoes) attack, avoiding a direct fleet confrontation until the odds were loaded strongly in their favour. Under the inspired leadership of Admiral William Sims, American Dreadnought construction went ahead rapidly from 1906.

The originality of thought in American battleship design, especially from 1905 to 1920, was a marked feature of this period. America's first Dreadnoughts, the *South Carolina* and *Michigan*, were markedly smaller than the British prototype of the breed, and attained a speed no higher than many pre-Dreadnoughts. But they were neat, carefully planned and economical, especially in the layout of their main armament of 12-inch guns.

Six Dreadnoughts followed this first American pair, armed with ten or twelve 12-inch guns. Then when Britain introduced the 13.5-inch gun, America went one better with the 14-inch, which first appeared in the *New York* and *Texas* laid down in 1911. Having pioneered super-imposition and a multitude

CENTRE (*above*): *The tough, highly efficient and fast (28 knots) German battle cruiser* Moltke *of the First World War*

CENTRE (*below*): *The Atlantic fleet, 1925, led by the battleship* Rodney

of features like the lattice mast (for strength, and rangefinder stability), American architects introduced a new defence feature in their 14-inch-gunned battleships laid down in 1912. Once before, at the height of the guns *versus* armour contest of the 1860s and '70s, designers had been forced to resort to concentrating all their armour weight over the ship's vitals. With the increasing penetrating and explosive power of the new 13.5- and 14-inch guns, it was evidently necessary to revert to a similar disposition of armour plate, unless the battleship were to sink under the weight of its own protective steel. With the *Oklahoma* and *Nevada* the American Navy took the plunge. When they were completed there was armour up to 18 inches thick on the turrets and their trunks, 16 inches on the conning tower, and over 13 inches in a narrow waterline belt and round the funnel base – and almost nothing anywhere else. Seven more 14-inch-gunned Dreadnoughts of up to 32,000 tons, all oil-fuelled and turbine-powered, were built between 1914 and 1921. This massive battleship programme was completed with a trio of 16-inch-gunned fighting ships, laid down in answer to the Japanese *Mutsu* and *Nagato*. Further, and still more hyperbolic super-battleships and battle cruisers, of over 40,000 tons and armed with twelve 16-inch guns, were authorized to meet the new Oriental super-battleships being built in Japan. Construction of these was halted in 1922; two of them, the *Saratoga* and *Lexington,* were completed as outsize aircraft carriers.

All the threat of bombs, all the proof by bombing trials of the vulnerability of the battleship to air attack, all the claims made by far-sighted theorists and prophets, could not deter the great powers from building battleships again as soon as they were allowed to by Treaty and felt themselves forced to by the imminence of a new war. The 'cult of the big bang' could not so easily be suppressed; the grandeur and imposing presence of the Dreadnought battleship provided more arguments in its favour than any mere theorizing could refute. The Dreadnought battleship had not done much fighting, it was true (a few minutes, without decision, at Jutland, that was about all), but its strategic influence had scarcely diminished in the minds of the world's defence councils when consideration had again to be given to battleship construction in the 1930s. All the great powers conformed. Between 1930 and 1940 Britain, America, Germany, Japan, France, Italy and Russia all laid down the keels of massive new battleships, varying in displacement from 25,000 to nearly 70,000 tons. The design of all these ships was mainly conservative, and the progress in naval architecture and scientific devices in the years preceding the Second World War did not come near to matching the astonishing achievements of 1906 to 1914. The increasing need to defend the vessel against bombing attack was seen in the large number of anti-aircraft guns, which could if necessary be used also against surface torpedo vessels, the number of aircraft carried on board (for reconnaissance, spotting and counter-attack), and the emphasis on the protection of the decks. The disposition of armour against shellfire generally followed the earlier American trend towards the all-or-nothing principle.

The French followed British practice for the first time, by concentrating all their heavy guns forward. They also reduced weight and expense by mounting four guns to a turret. Their *Dunkerque* and *Strasbourg*, *Richelieu* and *Jean Bart* could manage around 30 knots and were satisfactory enough fighting ships, but they lacked the old spark and originality. The other major powers conformed more closely to their own past tradition. Germany began before Hitler's time by flouting all the rules and laying down 'pocket battleships' which purported to be within the heavy cruiser Washington limit of 10,000 tons yet carried 11-inch guns, could do 26 knots with diesel engines, and had a radius of action of 10,000 miles. This combination of qualities seemed too good to be true, and so it was, for the *Deutschland* and her sisters actually displaced around 12,000 tons. Germany continued to concentrate on big fast capital ships for commerce raiding rather than ships to stand in the line as she had for the earlier war, and these reached their culmination in the enormously tough and formidable *Bismarck* and *Tirpitz* of some 42,000 tons armed with eight 15-inch guns. Italy built light and fast with her 35,000-ton *Roma*, *Littorio*, *Vittorio Veneto* and *Impero* (the last never completed), which were reputed to be capable of 35 knots but proved to be vulnerable to air attack. The airborne torpedo also demonstrated its deadly power against the *Prince of Wales*, one of the five new 35,000-tonners built by Britain between 1937 and 1942. Although equipped with enormous batteries of anti-aircraft guns of all calibres, they were not enough to fight off the swarming Japanese torpedo and high-level bombers on 10 December 1941: two torpedoes sufficed to cripple the battleship, and three more were quite sufficient to send her to the bottom.

After their savage losses by air attack at Pearl Harbor three days before the *Prince of Wales* went down, the Americans were quick to recognize the need to augment drastically their heavy ships' anti-aircraft defences. No nation built battleships of this last generation with such enthusiasm as the Americans. Between 1941 and 1944 ten 16-inch-gunned fighting ships – all immensely strong, very fast and up to 45,000 tons displacement – joined the fleet. Although conceived some thirty years later, they conformed to the design principles laid down by the Bureau of Construction for the old *Michigan* and *South Carolina*. The *Washington*, the *Alabama* and the *Missouri* were still Dreadnoughts. They were still basically gun-platforms, their single calibre heavy armament carried in three instead of four turrets. The main function of their armour plate was to resist enemy shell, their secondary batteries were to ward off other forms of high explosive carrier. But what batteries these were! By this time the aircraft carrier was the new capital ship of naval warfare. But when her aircraft came in to attack a Dread-

BELOW: *The Japanese battleship*, Yamato, *1941. On 4 July 1945 the* Yamato *blew up and sank after being struck by five bombs and ten torpedos*

OPPOSITE: *The USS* Alaska, *with nine 12-inch guns and a speed of 33 knots*

nought in the Pacific or the Mediterranean, they were met at once by the fire from 150 or more anti-aircraft guns of all calibres.

In the Second World War the American and British Dreadnoughts accepted with dignity their secondary rôle to the carrier. In the Mediterranean, Atlantic and Pacific they escorted convoys, bombarded shore positions, and acted as protective nursemaids to the carriers, filling the air with shot and shell when the enemy appeared in the sky. Not a single American battleship was lost between 1942 and 1945 to her old enemy, the gun, or to her new enemies, the aircraft bomb and torpedo. In her last great war, the battleship vindicated herself when she was properly protected against her new enemies by her own guns and by the command of the air provided by her new consort, the carrier. Without these advantages she was, by 1941, a hopelessly vulnerable fighting ship. The mighty *Tirpitz* succumbed to the bomb, her sister ship was first crippled and then finished off by the torpedo. In the Mediterranean, British and Italian battleships fell to bombs and torpedoes when command of the air was lost. In the Pacific, the Japanese fleet of battleships – some converted in desperation into semi-aircraft carriers – was whittled away by the dive bomber, the torpedo bomber, and on several occasions and for the last time, by enemy shellfire.

On 7 April 1945 the Japanese *Yamato* blew up and sank beneath a huge cloud of smoke at Leyte Gulf after being struck by some five bombs and ten torpedoes. The *Yamato* class of Japanese battleship were by a wide margin the largest and most heavily-gunned Dreadnoughts ever built: over 70,000 tons at full load, nine 18-inch guns in three triple turrets, and an 18-inch belt of armour and 22 inches on her turrets, speed 27 knots.

Surely the end of these giant Dreadnoughts, these *ne plus ultra* gun platforms, marked the final death of the battleship at the hands of the airplane? Not a bit of it. Almost since the original *Dreadnought* took to the sea, prophets had been announcing the demise of the battleship. But when the American navy, the largest in the world, needed gunpower for her Far East wars of the 1950s and 1960s, she dusted off the moth-balled giants she had kept in store and sent them to sea. Time and again these battleships justified themselves off Korea, bombarding supply lines, arsenals and troop concentrations. After it was all over, their damage was repaired and they were tucked away again.

But even then their life was not over. In the most desperate days of the Vietnam war, and after the F-III had proved itself an expensive fiasco, the *New Jersey* was recalled to the colours in 1966 – a battleship's guns to replace a bomber's bombs! In 1967 the refitted and modernised *New Jersey* steamed magnificently down the Delaware and off to the war, surely the last Dreadnought ever to do so? What is more, she did excellent service, her nine computerized big guns firing shells up to thirty miles with devastating accuracy and in all weathers. It was said that their arrival, without warning or means of counter-action, caused shock and distress as well as frightful damage.

The Battle Cruiser

This class of twentieth-century fighting ship was the natural twin of the Dreadnought battleship. The cruiser version sacrificed armour and guns for greater speed and replaced the armoured cruisers as a fast scouting force attached to the main battle fleet. They were magnificent looking ships at their full speed of 25 to 30 knots firing a full broadside of heavy guns. The British built them with bigger guns and less structural strength than the Germans in the First World War, and paid the price. Three blew up at Jutland. The Japanese built battle cruisers, too. They went out of fashion between the World Wars, and were briefly revived in 1944.

The Aircraft Carrier

Of all the new weapon-carriers the aircraft has remained, even to this day, the most restricted in its endurance. In the early days of the torpedo, 'mother ships' had been fitted out expressly to carry very small torpedo boats for launching within close range of the enemy – preferably at night. When, after a number of experiments by German, British and Italian pioneers, the first practical torpedo-carrying aircraft rose from the water (it was a seaplane) in 1914, and Winston Churchill as First Lord of the Admiralty authorized the construction of a flight of them, means were already being considered for extending their range. The seaplane carrier, like the torpedo boat carrier of forty years earlier, provided the solution.

The British were the leading pioneers in the development of a naval air arm. In May 1912 a naval air service was formed. In 1913 a half-completed merchant-ship was bought and converted to carry seaplanes, which were hoisted out by crane, dropped in the sea, and even more hazardously recovered after they had landed again. Later, much faster ships which could keep up with the fleet at sea were similarly converted, and one of these was employed with the British Grand Fleet at Jutland. The Germans at first backed the airship against the heavier-than-air machine, but were soon to recognize the benefits of the smaller, cheaper and nimbler aircraft.

The seaplane carrier was always a makeshift vessel, limited in its capacity for carrying aircraft and in the conditions under which it could operate. It was obviously a much better idea to *launch* aircraft straight into the air while the carrier was moving. The first take-offs from ships were made in Britain and in America before the First World War. At first short runways were built on the forecastle of battleships. The British Navy built them on top of gun turrets, which could be conveniently turned into wind to shorten the take-off run. Spotting as well as fighter aircraft were employed in this way, and by the end of the war the Grand Fleet could launch as many as 120 aircraft into the air from its carriers, battleships and cruisers and from rafts towed behind fast destroyers.

The next stage of development was to provide a flight deck long enough for pilots to land their aircraft back on board so that the parent vessel did not have to stop to pick them up. Several British ships were converted for this purpose while still under construction. The Italian liner *Conte Rosso* and the Chilean battleship *Almirante Cochrane*, building in Britain, the battle cruiser *Furious* and the cruiser *Cavendish*, were all given long flight decks. Early in 1918, the world's first ship to be designed 'from scratch' as an aircraft carrier, the 11,000-ton *Hermes*, was laid down on the Tyne. She was the archetype of all the numerous carriers built by the great naval powers over the next fifty years – tall, ungainly, lopsided, with a flush deck extending from stem to stern; hangars below decks, lifts to raise the aircraft to their flying deck; mast, superstructure, bridge and

ABOVE: *The* Furious *receiving naval airship S.S.Z. (submarine scout). The* Furious *could carry a squadron of aircraft and an airship*

OPPOSITE: *One of the surprise-novelties of the First World War –the seaplane carrier and depot ship* Glorious

funnel reduced to a minimum and placed on the extreme starboard to allow her planes a clear run; guns for defence against aircraft and light surface attack; high speed to reduce to a minimum the length of take-off run. The duties of her aircraft included submarine spotting and destroying, reconnoitring, bombing and torpedoing the enemy, and fighting off similar attack.

In the period between the wars the aircraft carrier acquired growing status. The capital ship of the fleet remained the battleship. But the rapid improvement in speed, range, and destructive potential of the aircraft between 1916 and 1919 proved in numerous bomb and torpedo trials after the war, and the 'battleship holiday' enforced by the Washington Treaty, caused many of the great naval powers to give greater attention to their air arm. Japan, deprived by Treaty of parity in battleships with America, converted some of her forbidden half-

completed giant battleships and battle cruisers into vast and fast floating airfields with horizontal funnels. The United States replied by carrying out a similar conversion to the uncompleted hulls of her aborted 35,000-ton battle cruisers, *Lexington* and *Saratoga*, which could carry at 34 knots a hive of around a hundred aircraft, were modestly armoured, and were capable of defending themselves with the gunpower of a heavy cruiser. The French Ministry of Marine also took the uncompleted hull of a battleship and turned it into the ugly, box-like and rather slow carrier *Béarn*. By the outbreak of war again, Britain had seven carriers in commission, and another half dozen large fleet carriers building. Shortly before his death in 1920, the prophetic Fisher had written, 'By land and sea the approaching prodigious aircraft development knocks out the present fleet, makes invasion practicable, cancels our country being an island, and transforms the atmosphere into the battleground of the future ....' By the end of the 1920s it was beginning to appear that the old admiral's last prophecy – like so many of his earlier ones – was coming to pass. In the British, American and Japanese navies, aircraft bombing and torpedoing at sea was becoming an advanced and

ABOVE: *The USS* America *CVA 66*

OPPOSITE: *The USS* Ranger *CVA 61 and the USS* England *DLG 22 (out of sight) refuelling from the USS* Sacramento *AOE 1. Ships can again stay at sea indefinitely, as they did in Nelson's day*

sophisticated business. The Japanese especially spent heavily on the building of carriers, carrier aircraft and weapons, and the training of flying crews. By 1941 Japan possessed the most powerful and advanced fleet air arm in the world, manned by skilful and dedicated air crews: by airpower alone, it crippled the American Pacific Fleet on 7 December 1941; and from that date until the conclusion of hostilities in 1945, through the desperate combats at Coral Sea, Midway, Guadalcanal, and Leyte Gulf, the torpedo- and dive-bomber (with the submarine) ruled the Pacific, while the carrier was tenderly guarded by her own aircraft, by destroyers and cruisers, and by the Dreadnoughts she had replaced as queen of the fleet. In the first half of 1942 Japanese naval power – through its superbly efficient air arm – dominated the waters of the Pacific and Indian Oceans. When American aircraft in their turn destroyed four Japanese fleet carriers at the Battle of Midway, America within a few hours had regained maritime control because she had achieved control of the air above the sea's surface.

The Americans, Japanese and British all converted ships for carrier use and built new carriers in great numbers. All sorts of makeshifts were resorted to in order to get more aircraft into the air. Turrets were stripped from battleships to make room for runways. More and more aircraft for catapult launching were carried on warships, and even merchantmen. British merchantmen were equipped with a single fighter which could be launched against bombers, the pilot later parachuting into the sea close to his mother ship. Prolonged and bloody campaigns remained to be fought, and many American ships and aircraft were to be destroyed in the years ahead; but from

that day in June 1942 at Midway there could be no other outcome than victory for the Americans and their allies.

The introduction from 1945 of jet-powered aircraft with very high wing loadings, and therefore high landing speeds, complicated the problem of 'landing on', always the most difficult and dangerous aspect of carrier flying. Nets and hooks to reduce the landing run had been used since the early days of the carrier, even for slow piston-engined biplanes. The simple remedy now was to 'angle' the flight deck. Take-off was assisted by steam catapults.

It has been argued, especially in Britain where the economy is so precariously poised and defence costs are so high, that the carrier will be as obsolete in the 1970s as the battleships in the 1940s; that the carrier aircraft's duties can be more economically and effectively taken over by shore-based aircraft. The Americans on the other hand continue to pin much faith in the monster carrier – vast, nuclear-powered vessels with an unlimited endurance. They carry a complement of over 4,000 officers and men and supersonic bombers and fighters, and are protected by every conceivable form of anti-aircraft, anti-missile and anti-submarine device. They are even secure against nuclear fall-out. Although we all pray that sea warfare will never again occur, the construction of such super-carriers make it certain that the long history of the fighting ship will continue.

Index